MINIMALIST DESIGNS·1
COLORING·BOOK

ARTIST · INFO

ISBN-13: 978-1717404541

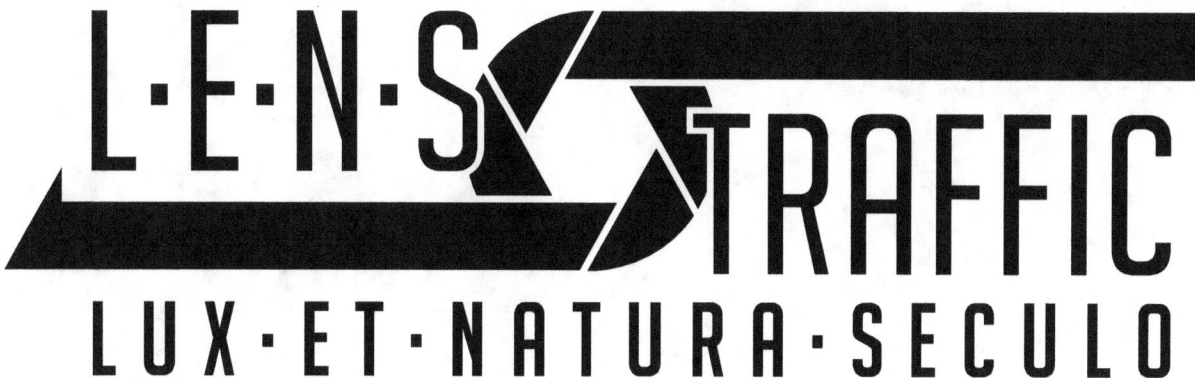

L·E·N·S TRAFFIC

LUX·ET·NATURA·SECULO

ALL PAGES ARE CENTERED
BETWEEN EDGE AND DOTTED LINE
CUT ALONG DOTTED LINE TO REMOVE

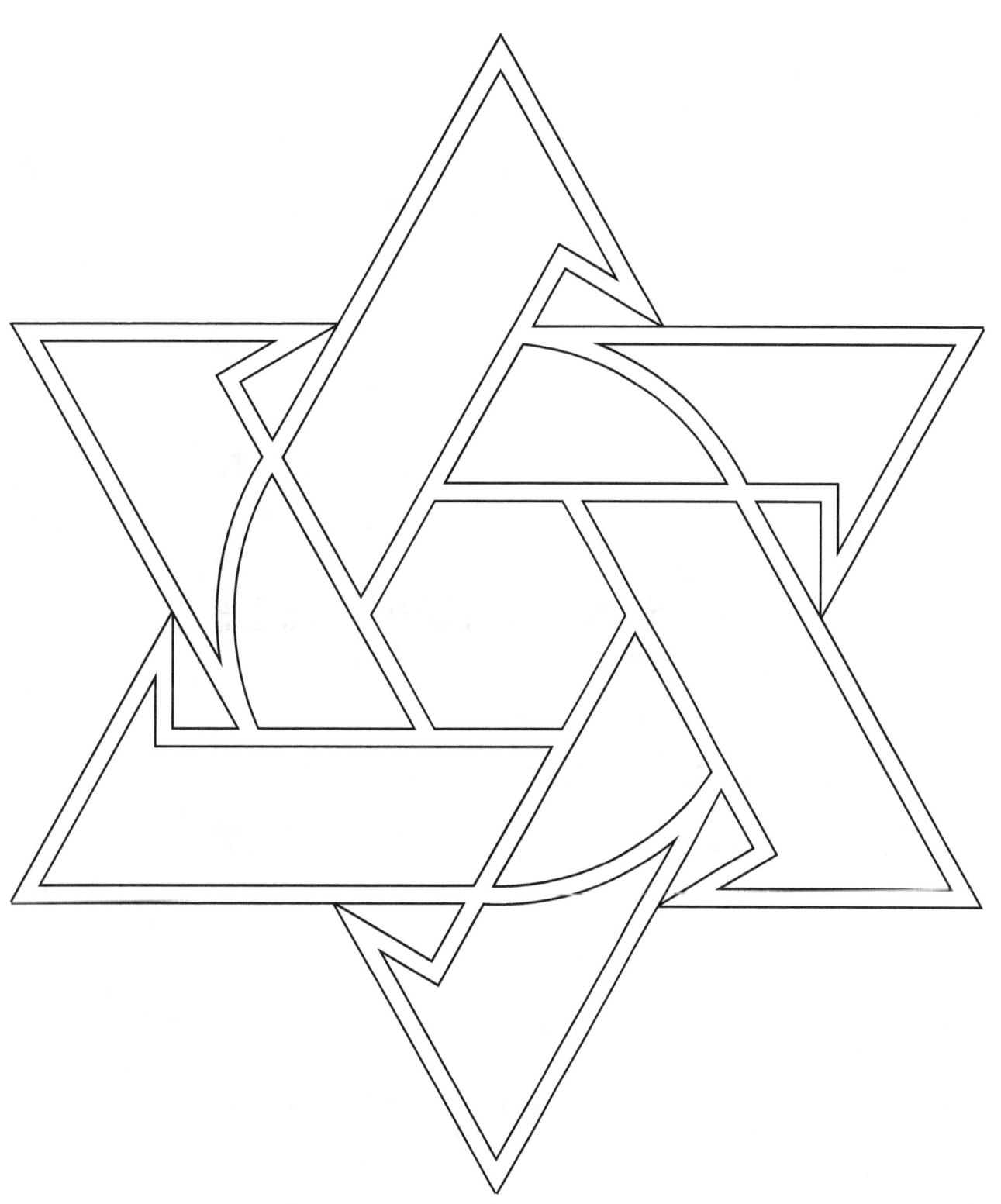

THIS IS YOUR TEST PAGE

TRY-OUT PENCILS, PENS, MARKERS, PAINTS, ETC.

PLACE BLANK PAPER BETWEEN PAGES TO PREVENT BLEED-THROUGH

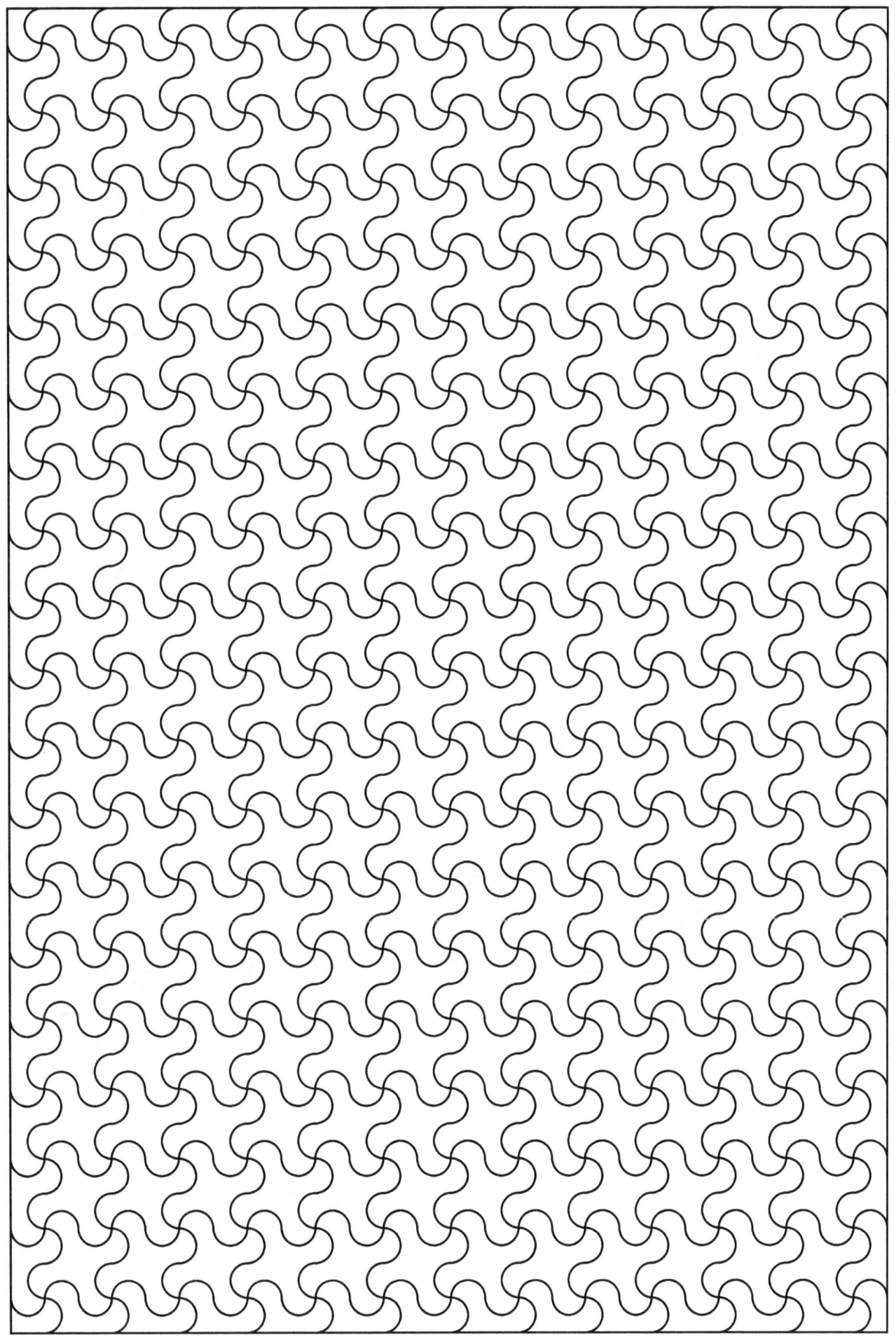

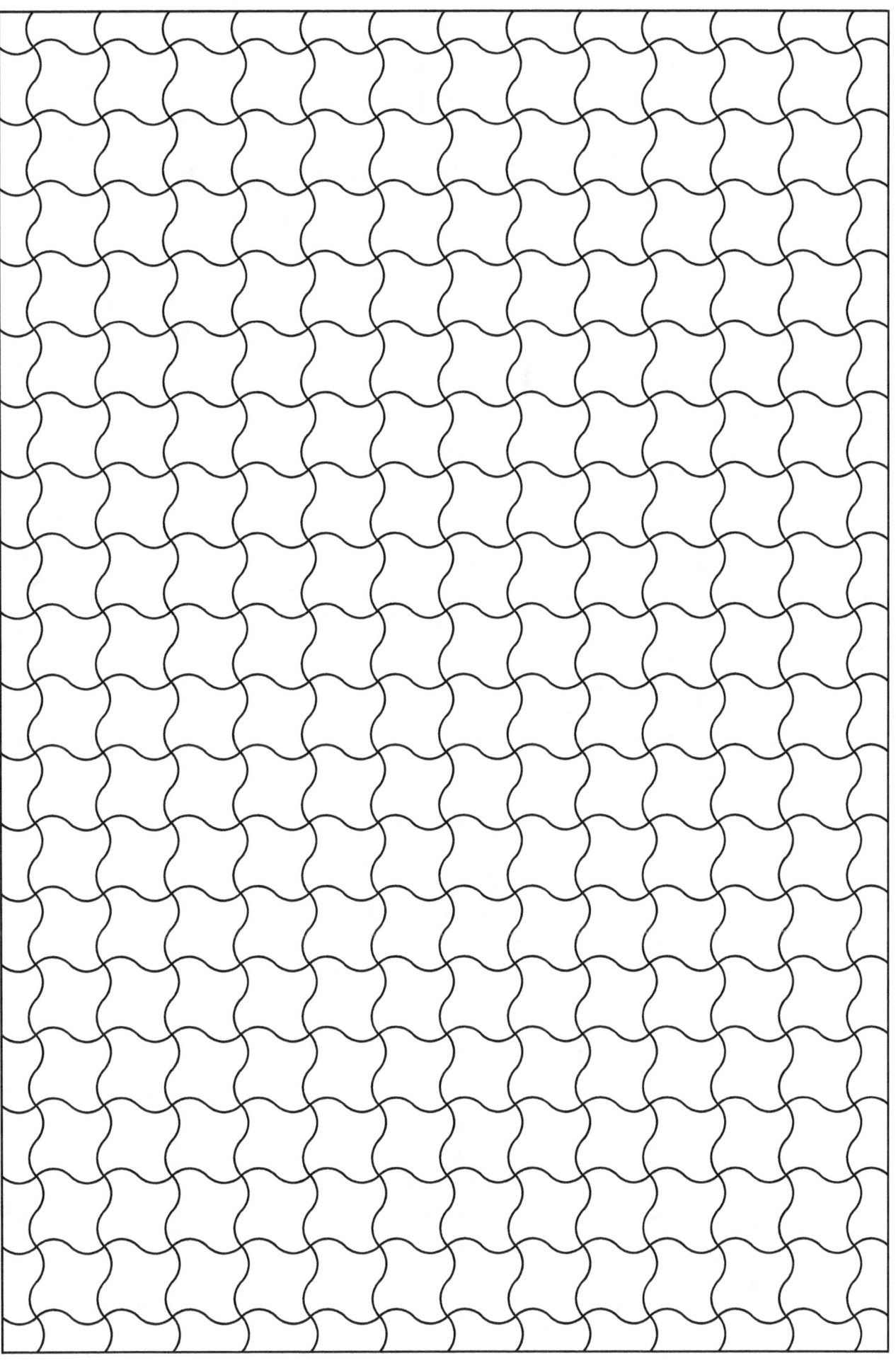

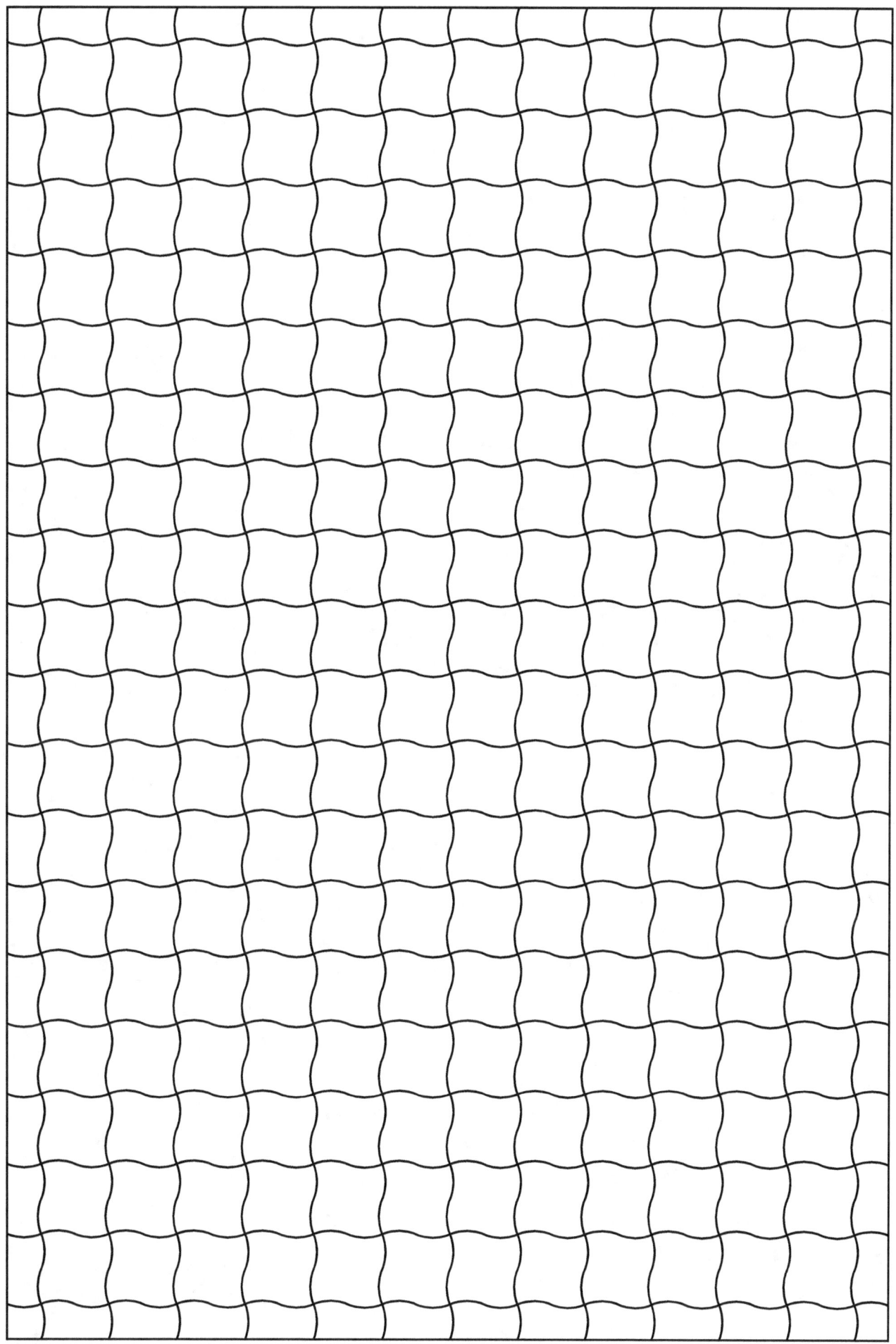

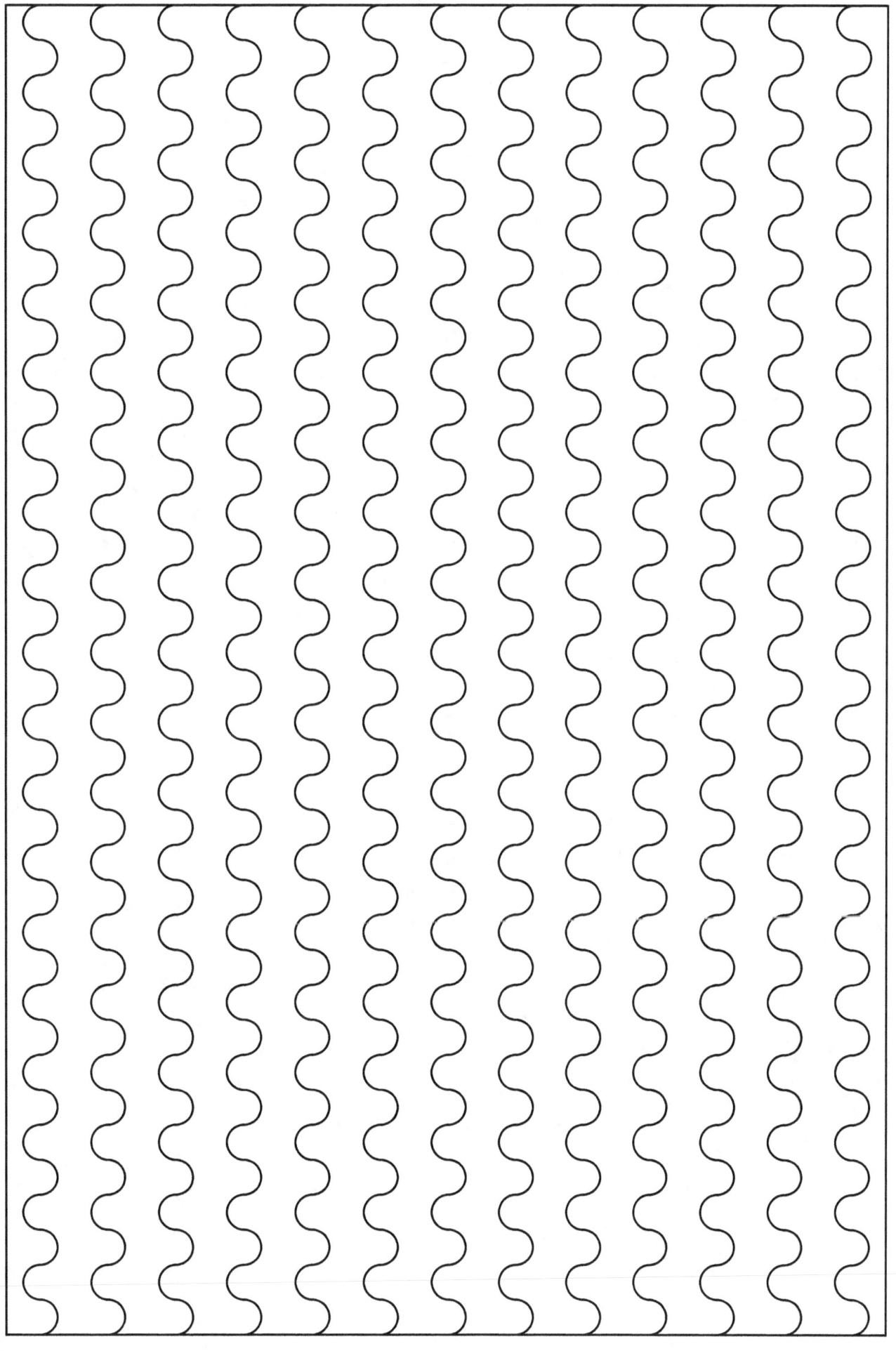

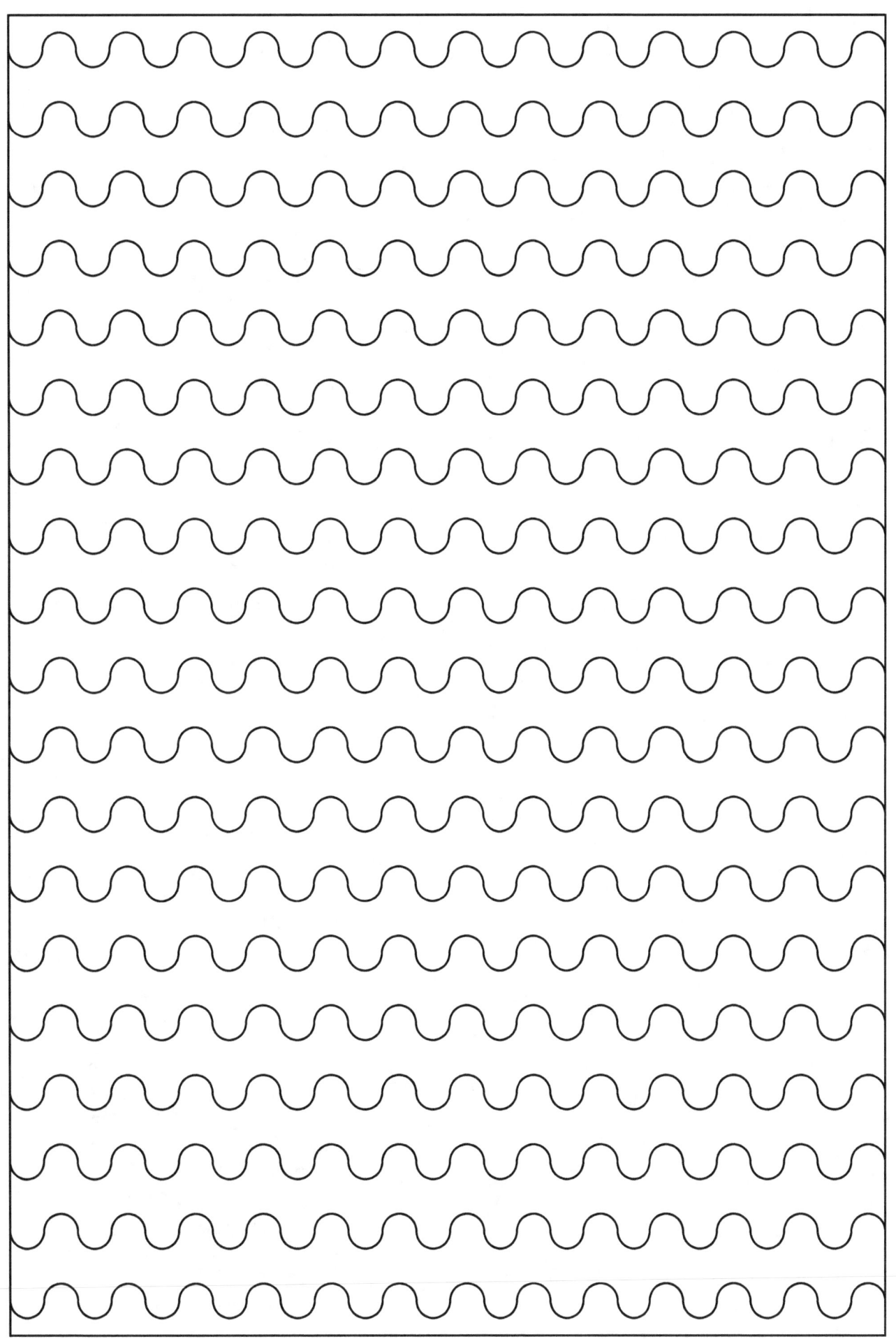

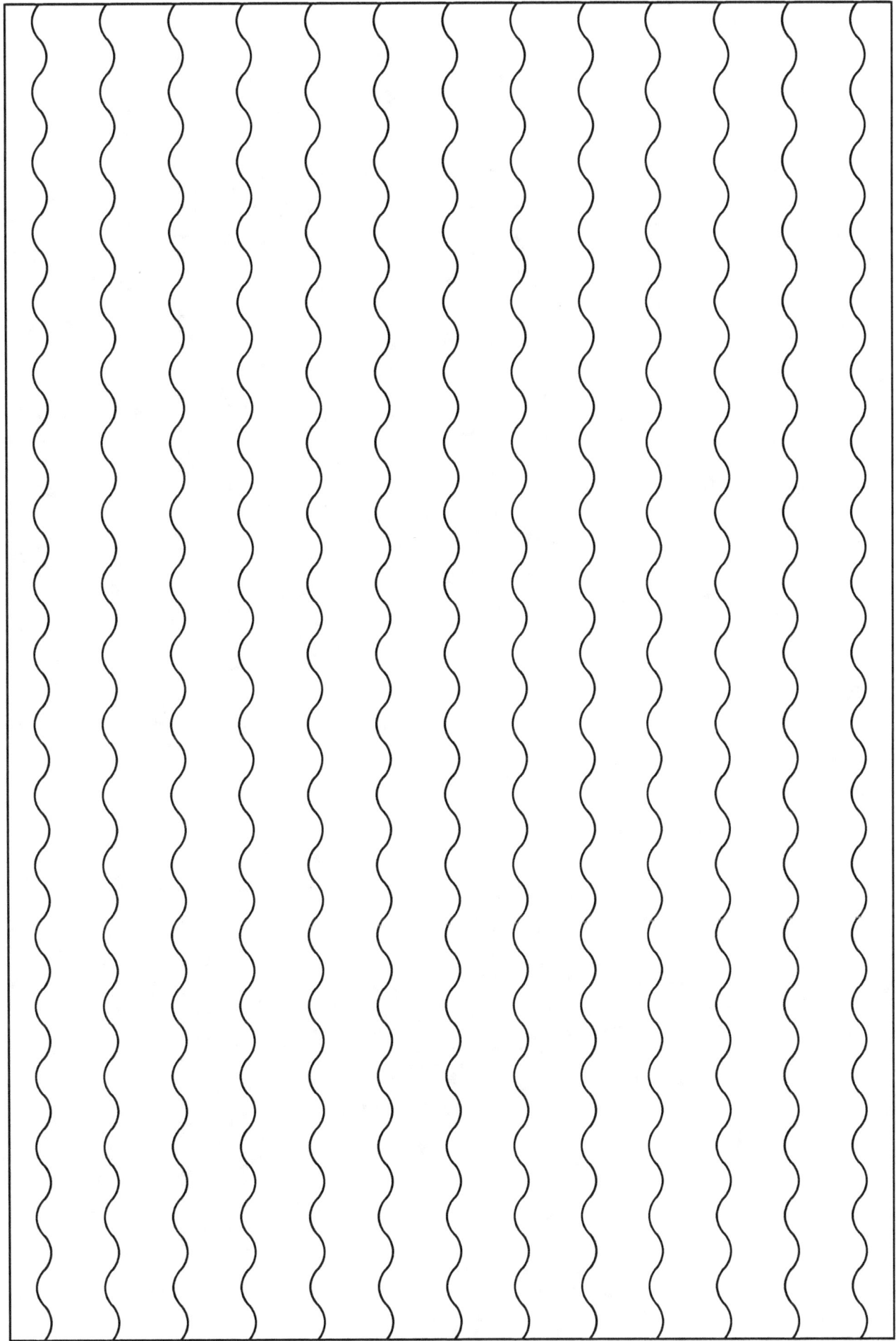

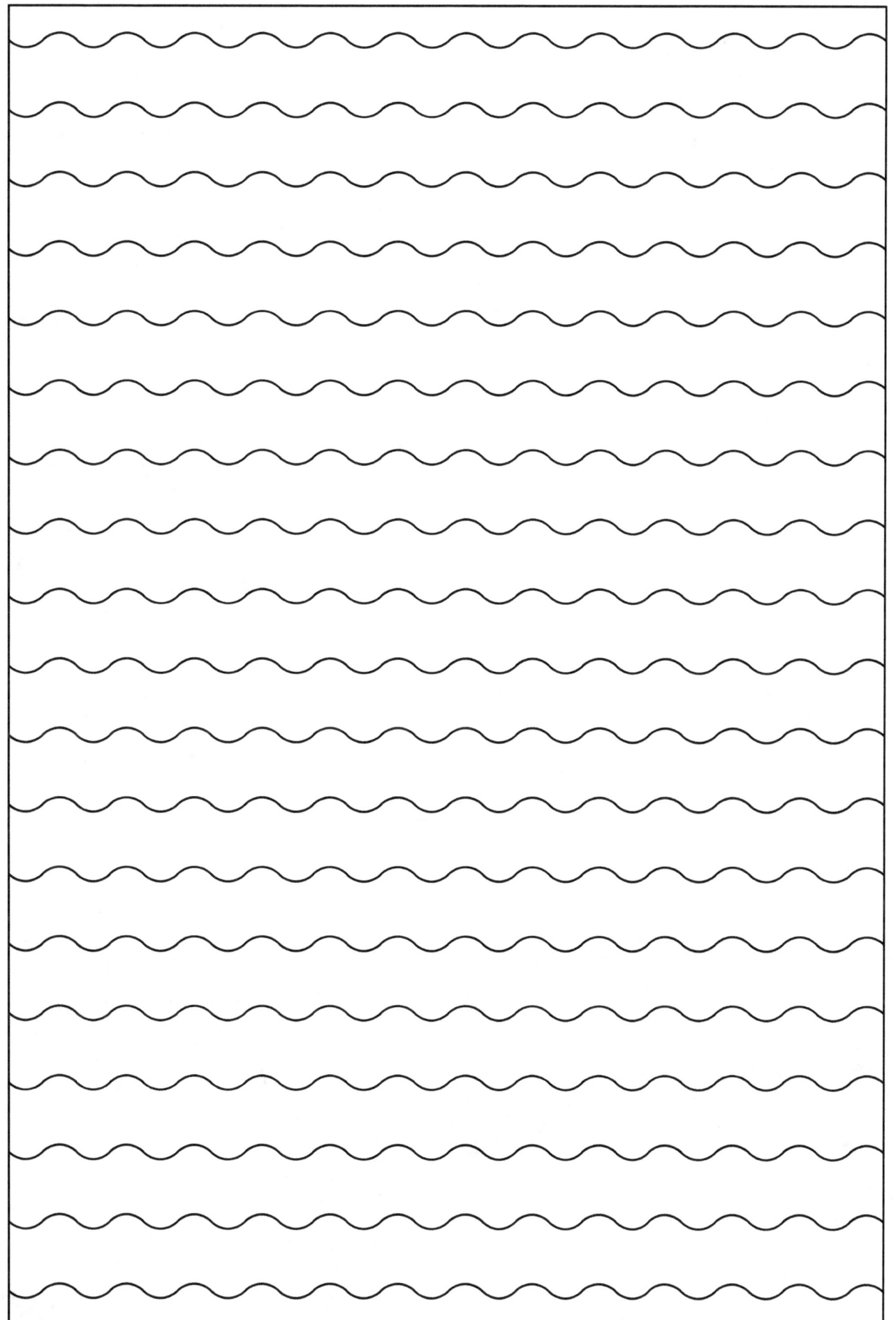

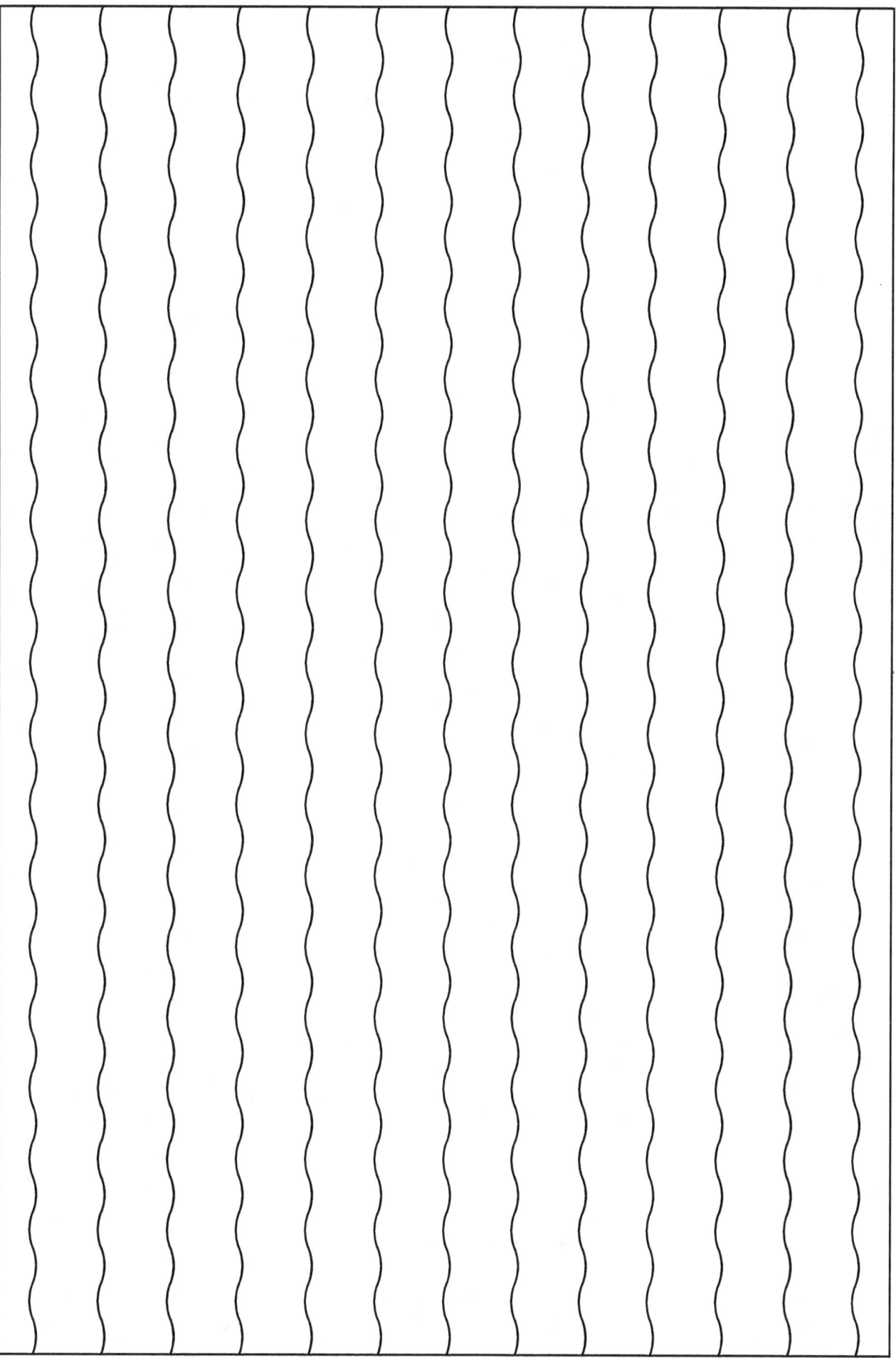

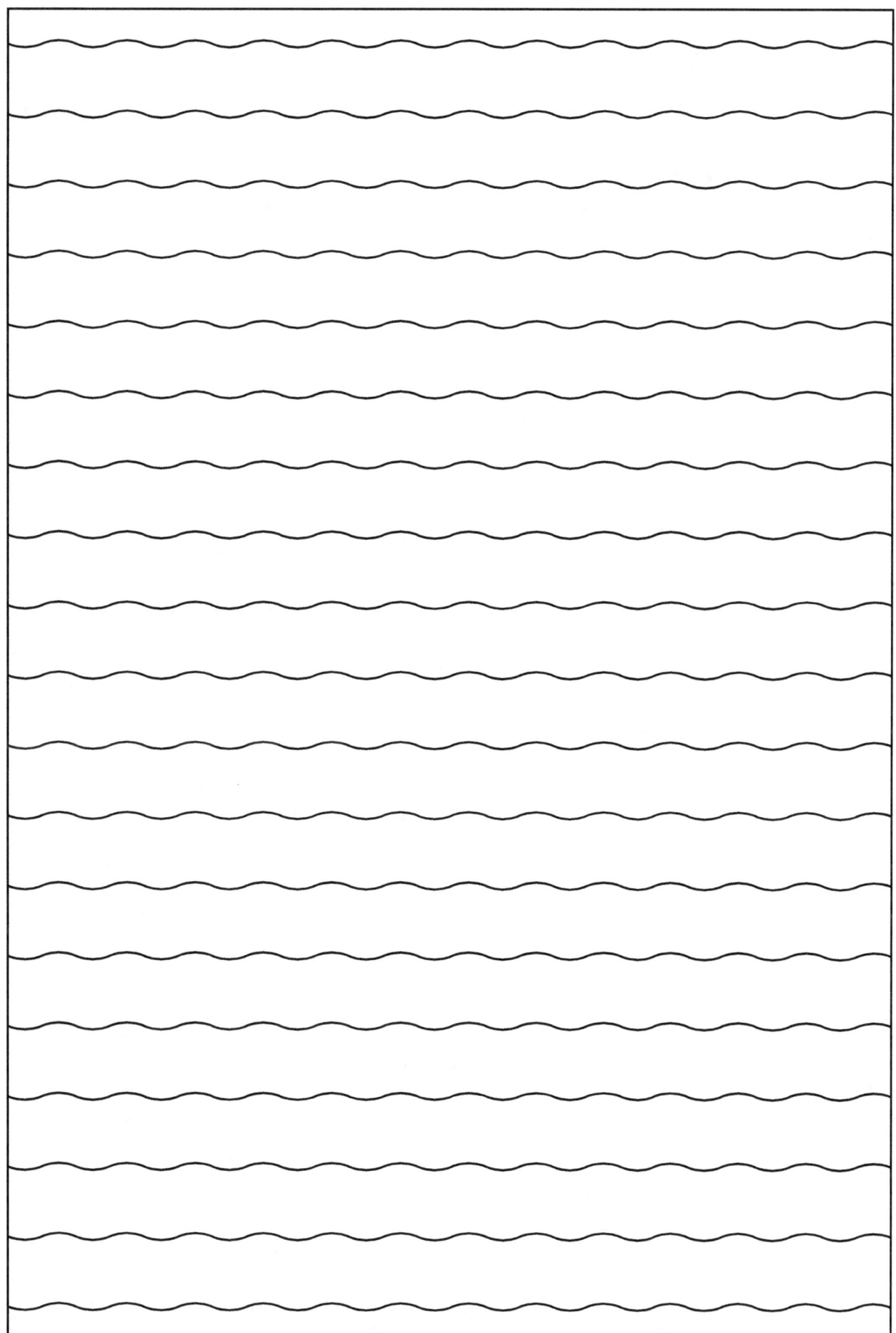

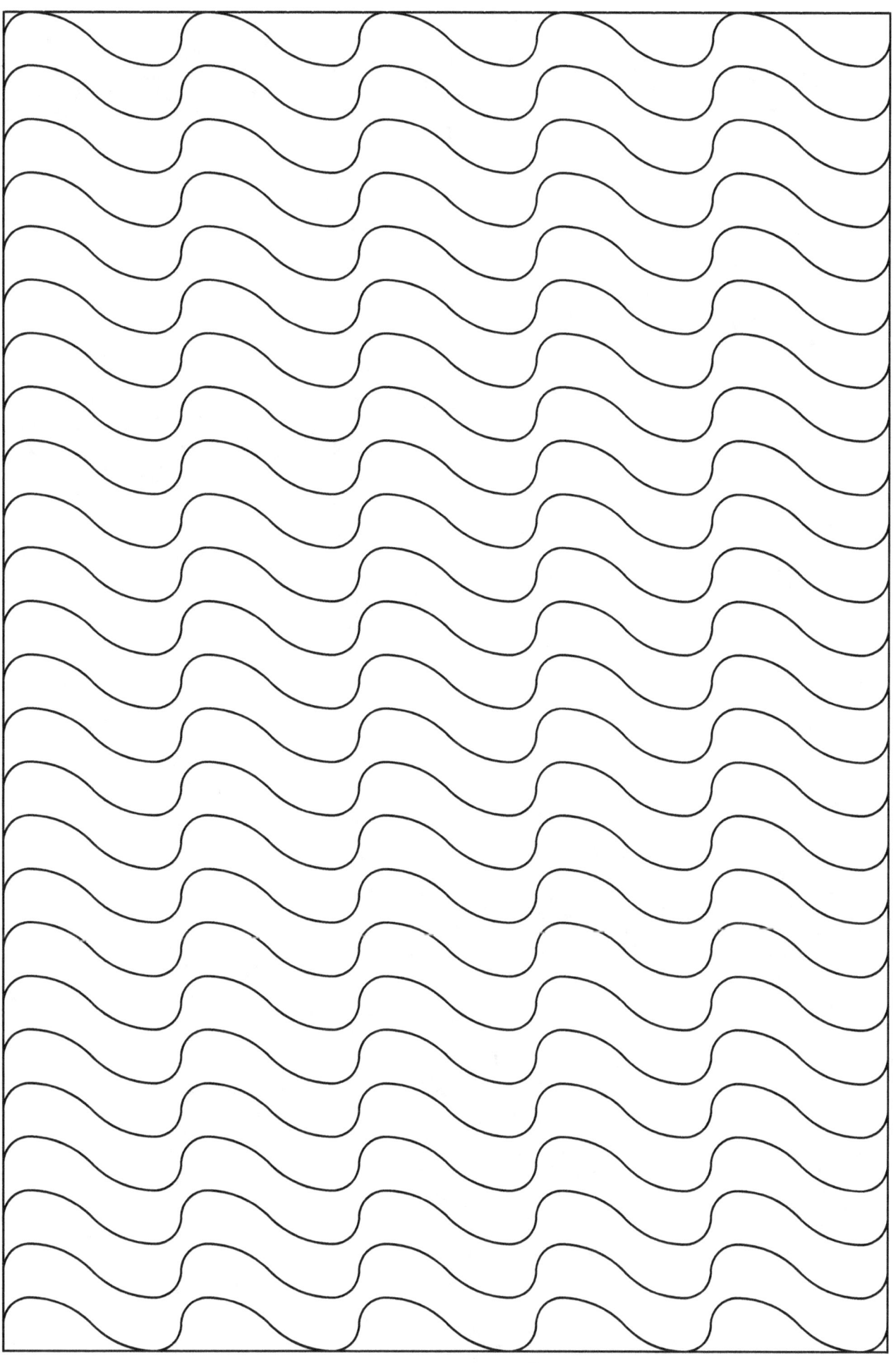

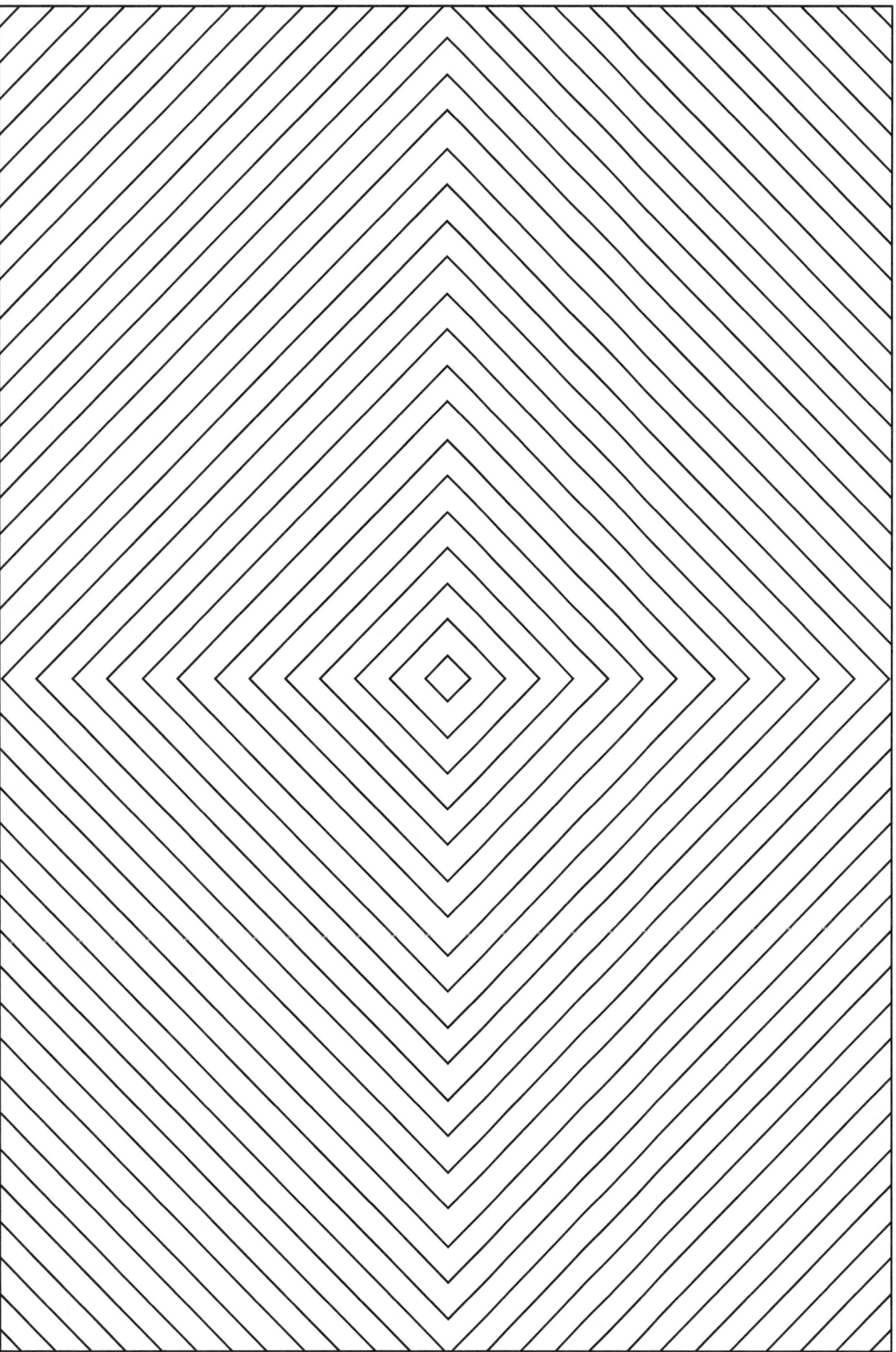

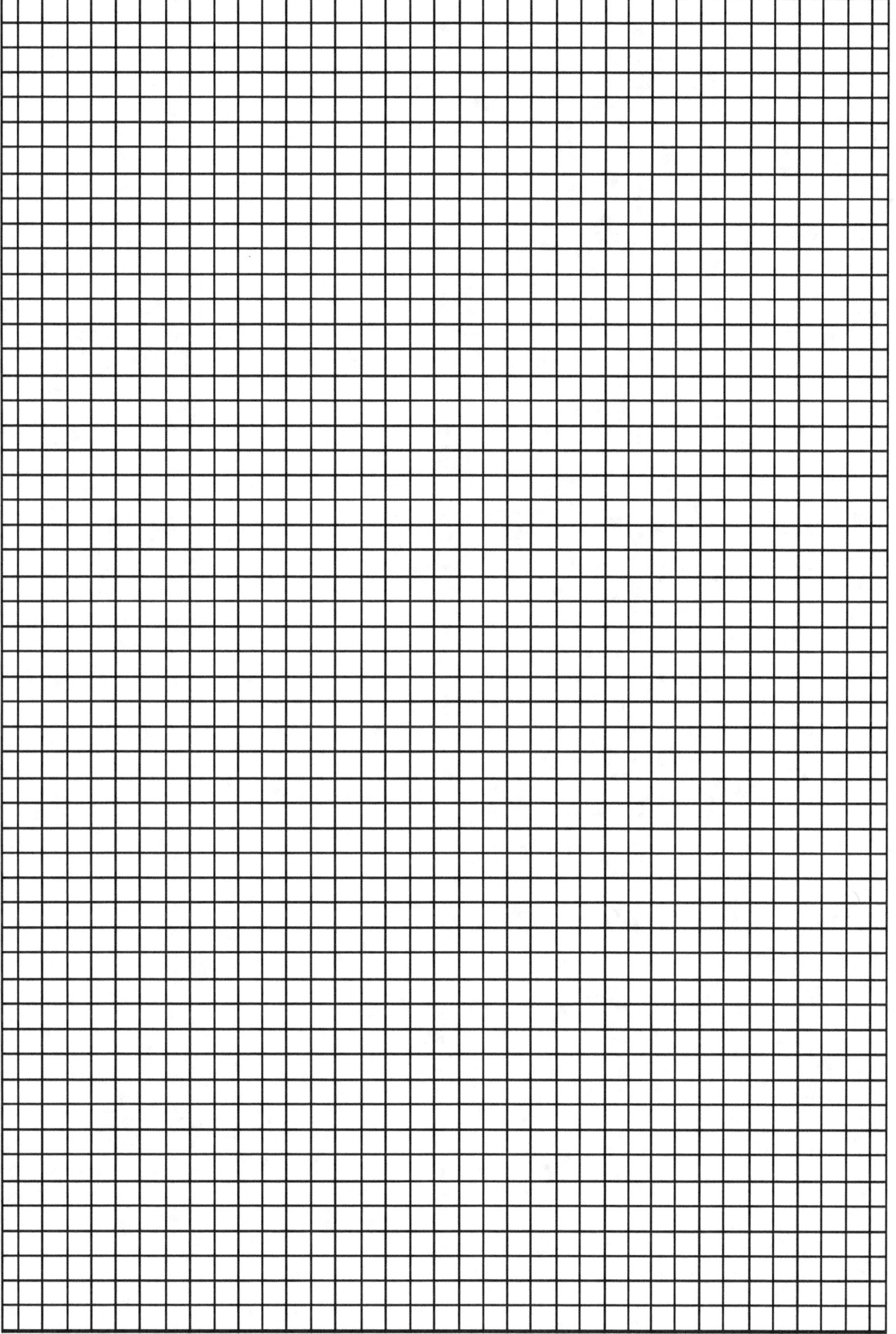

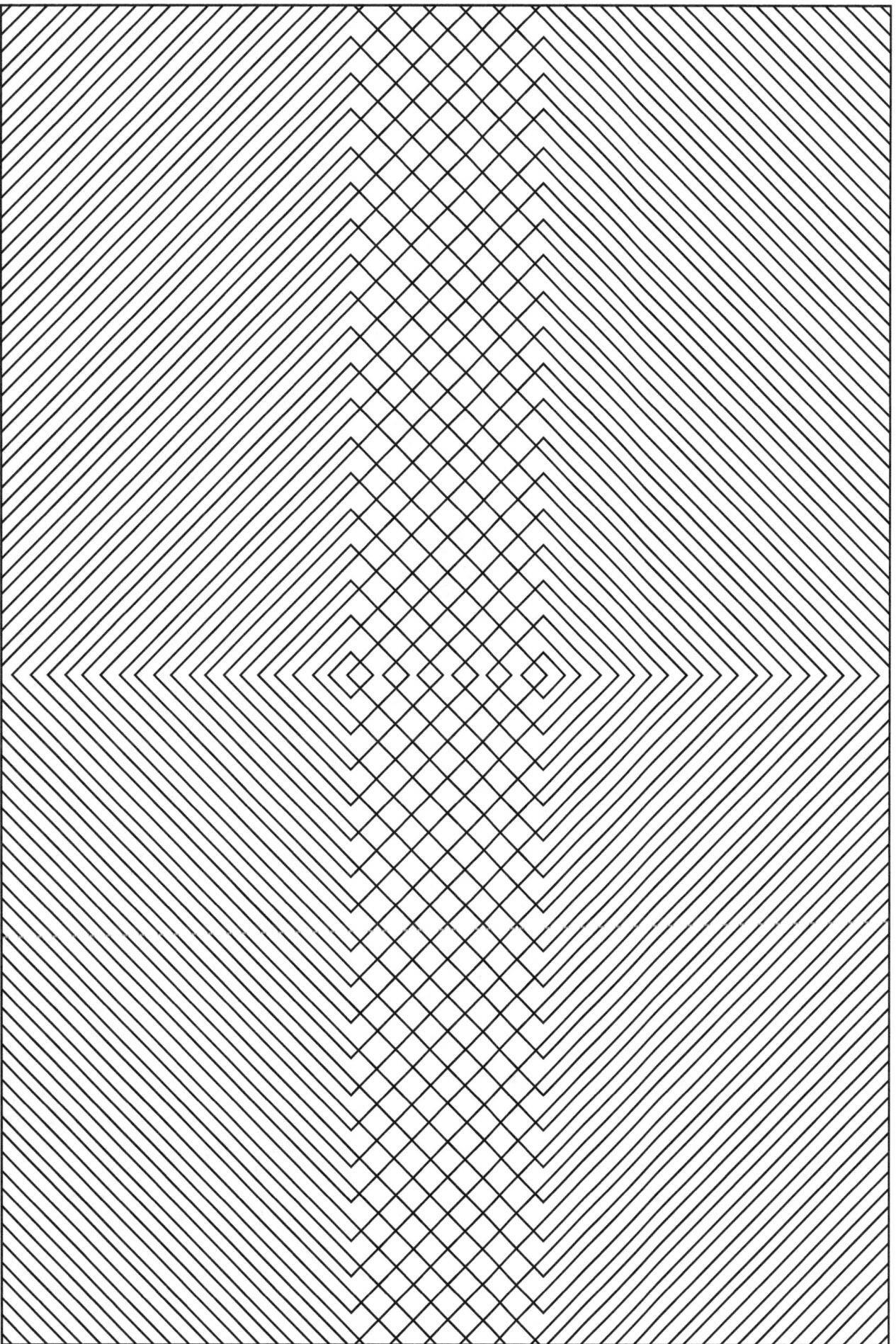

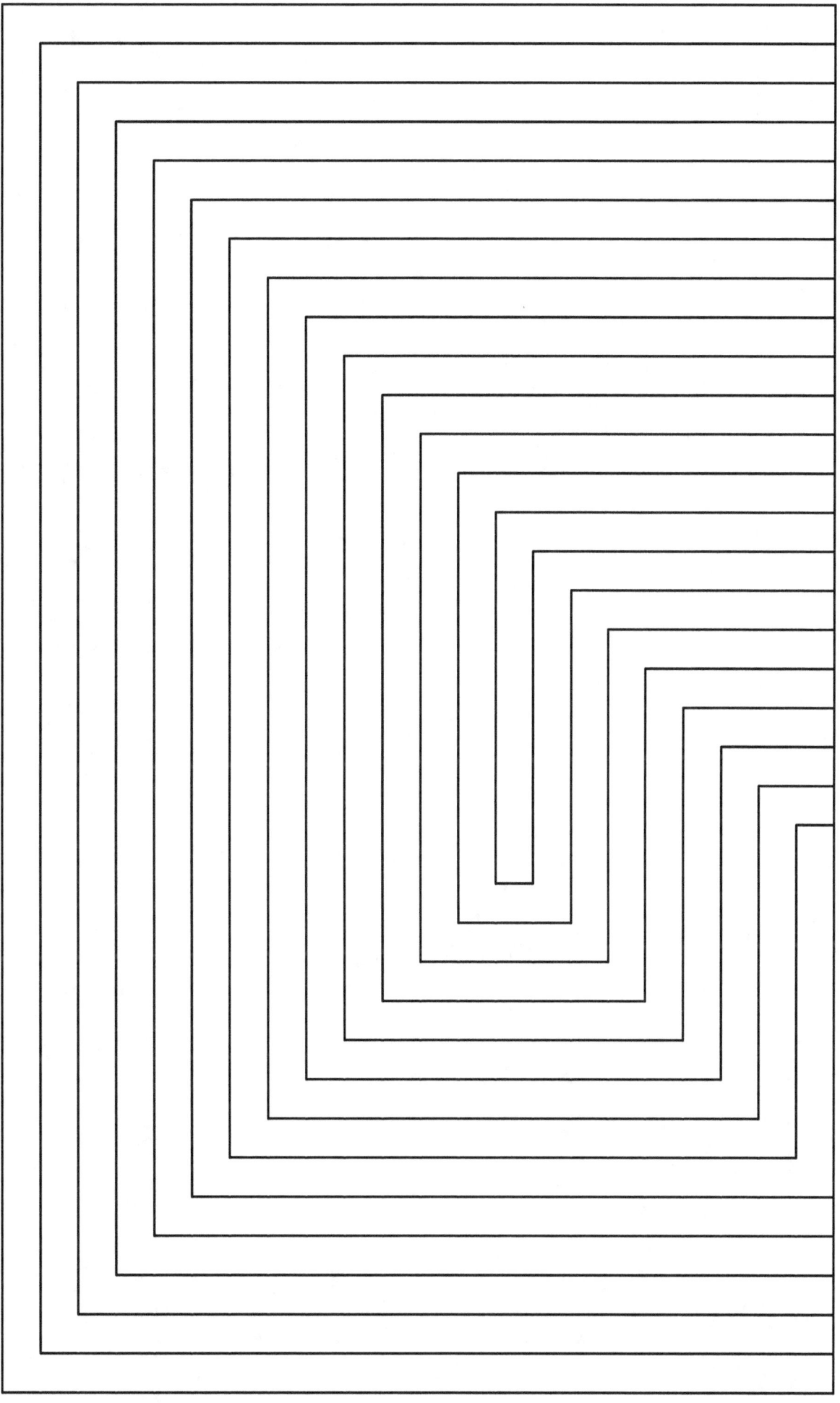

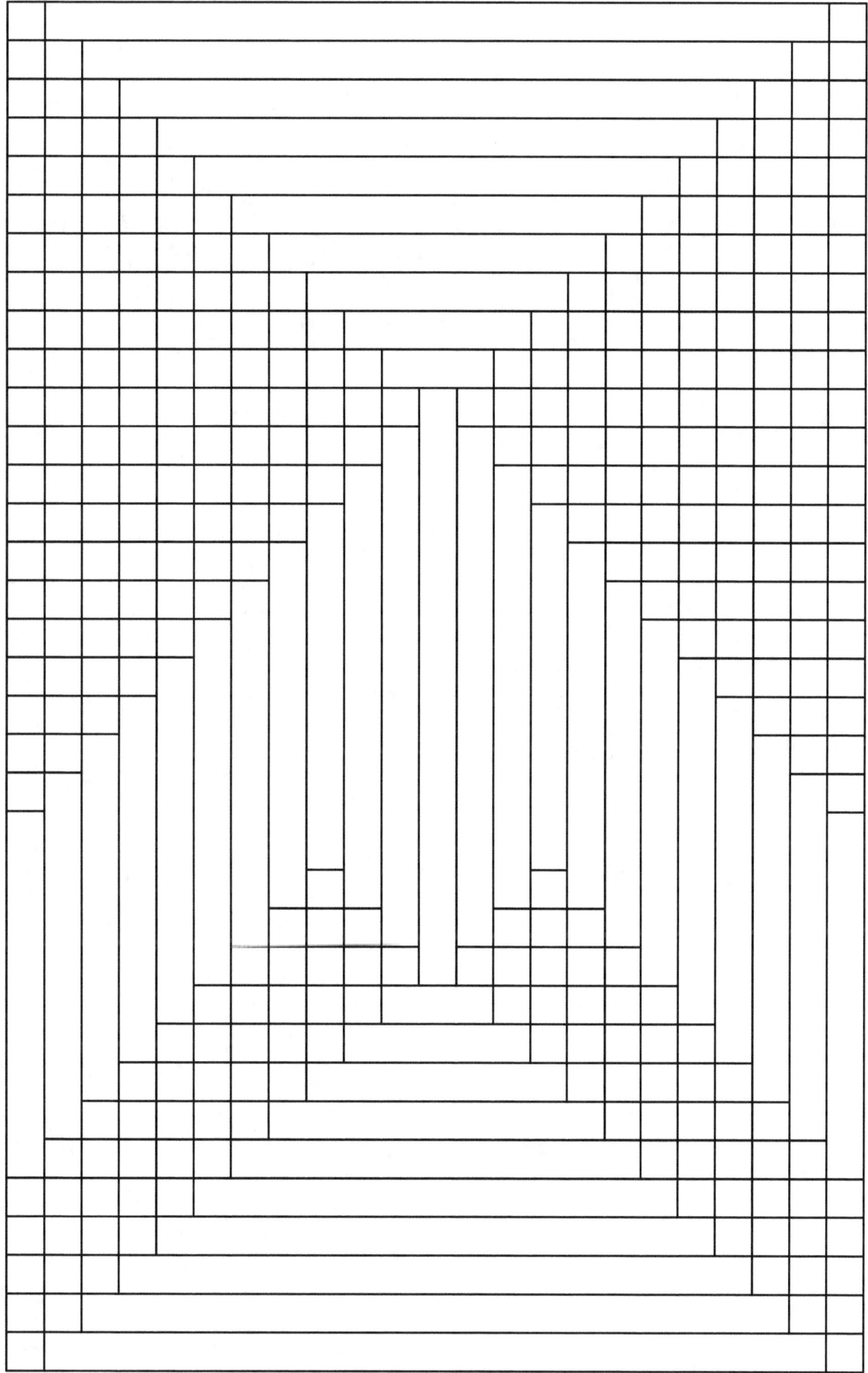

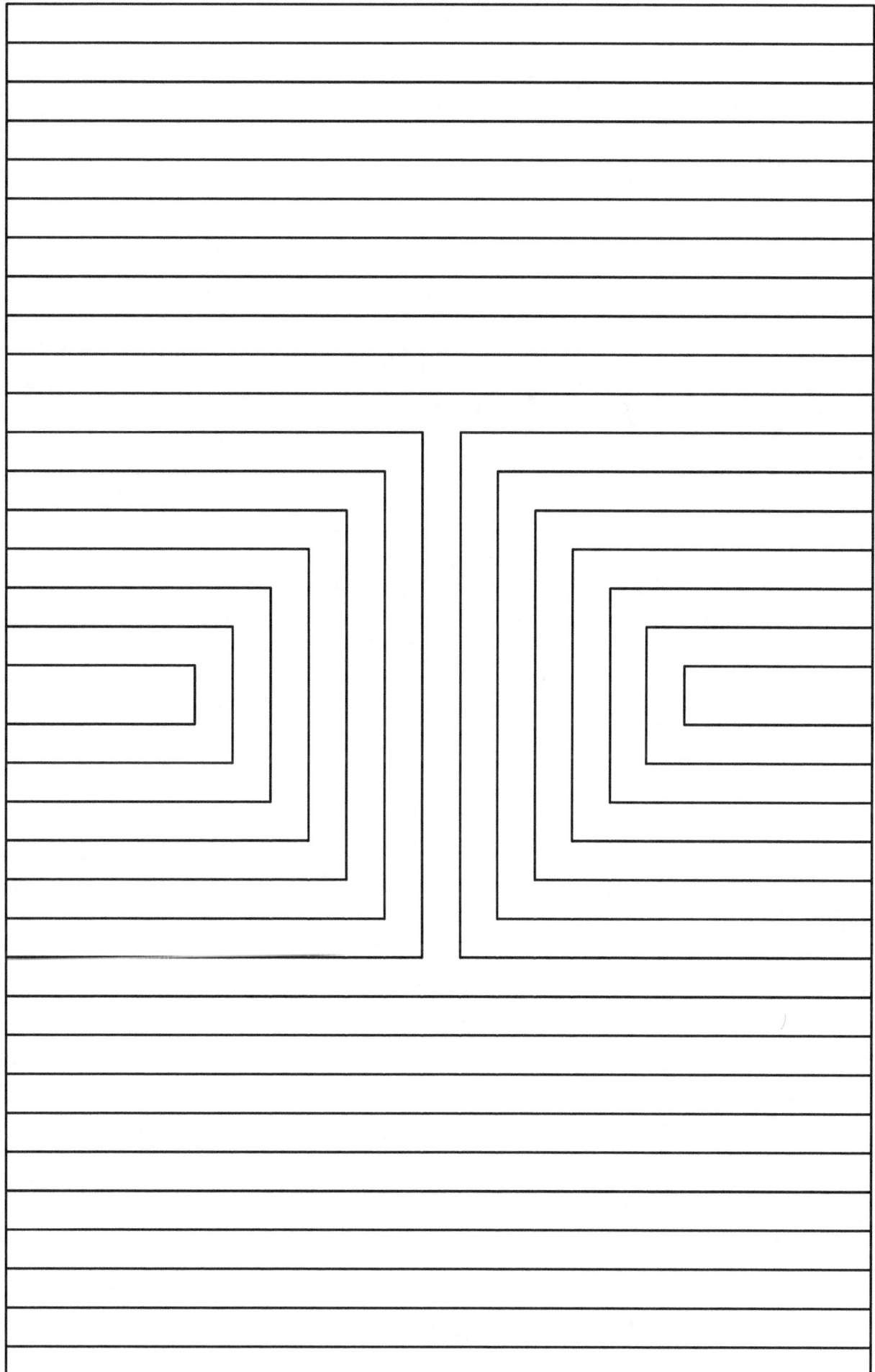

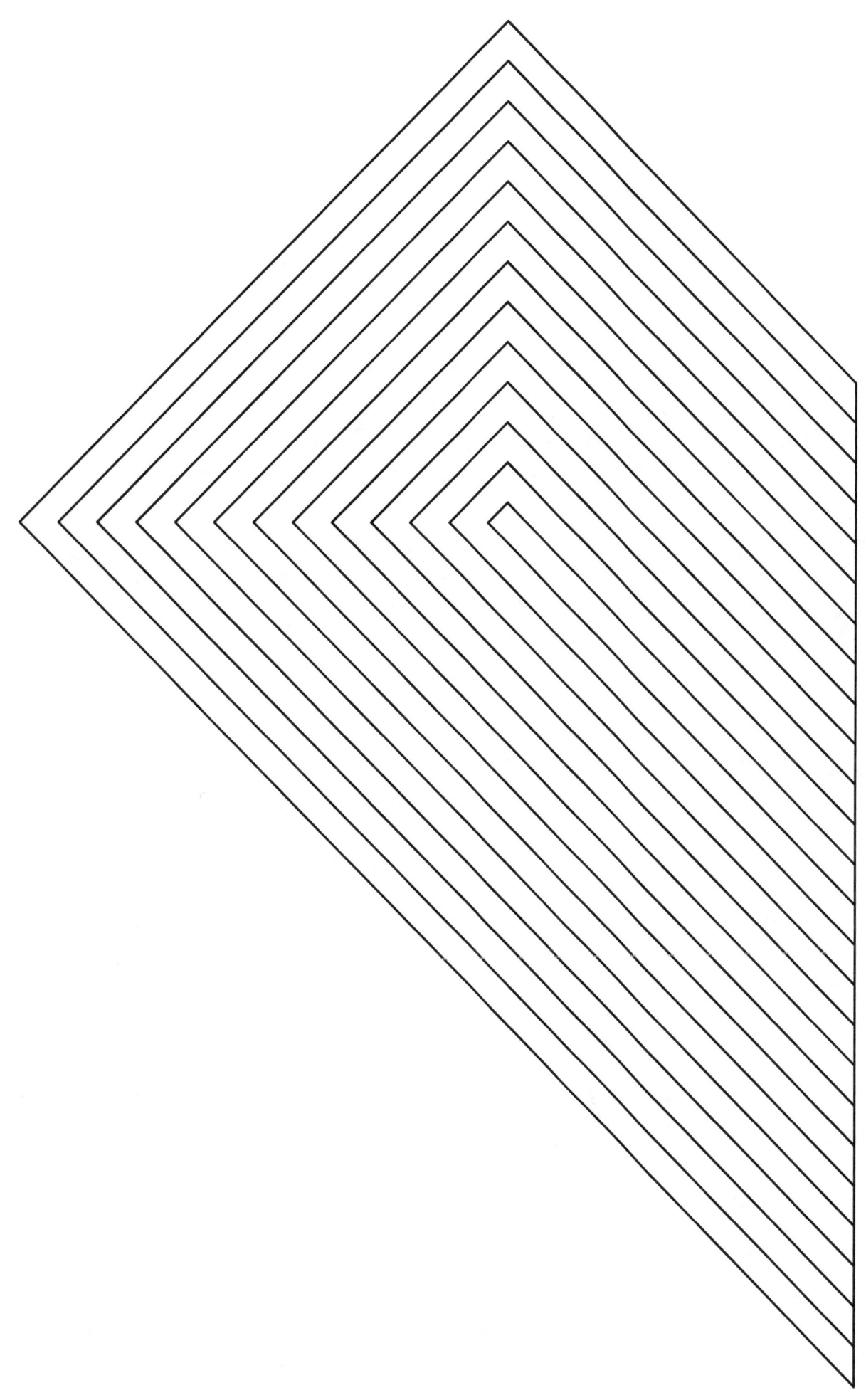

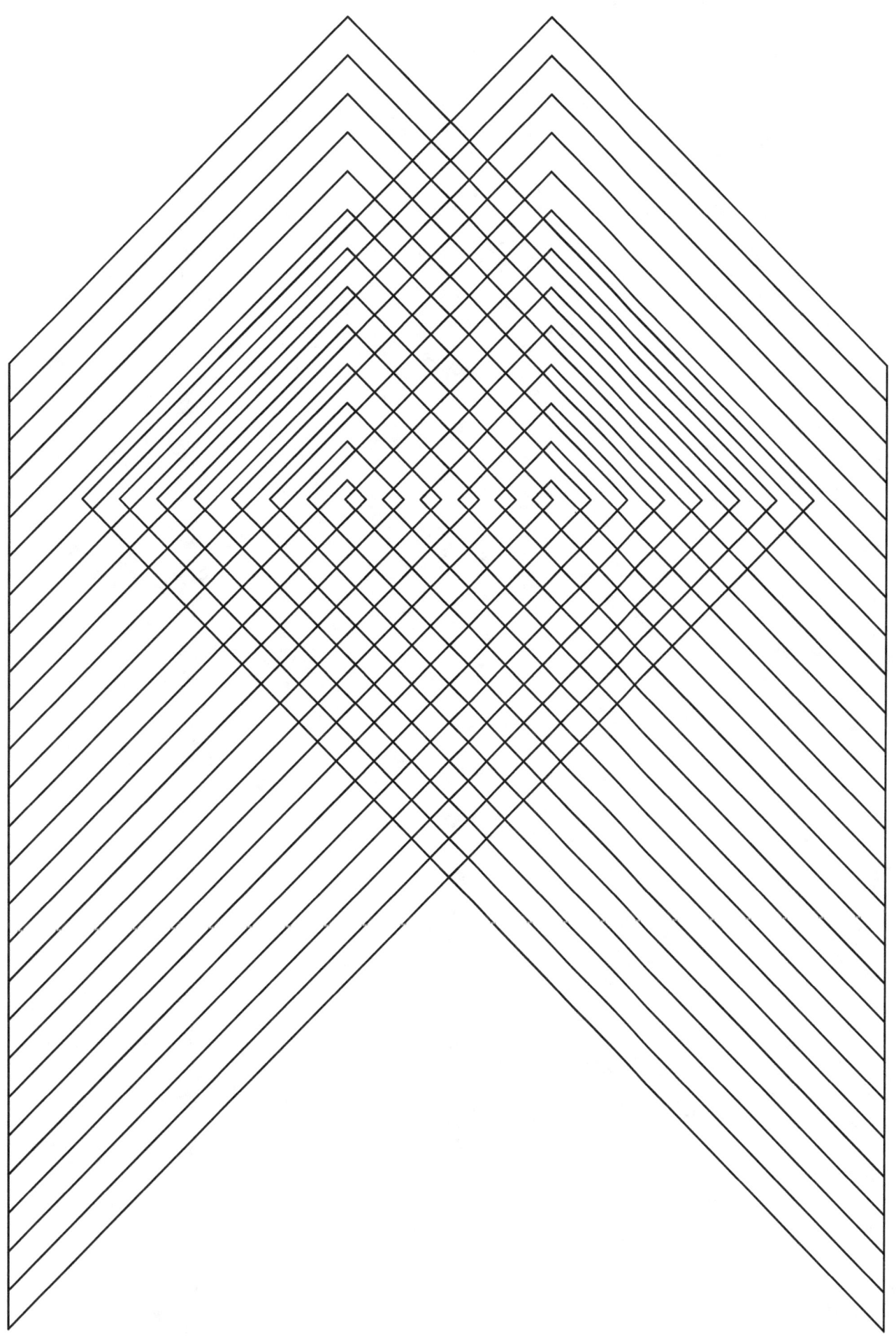

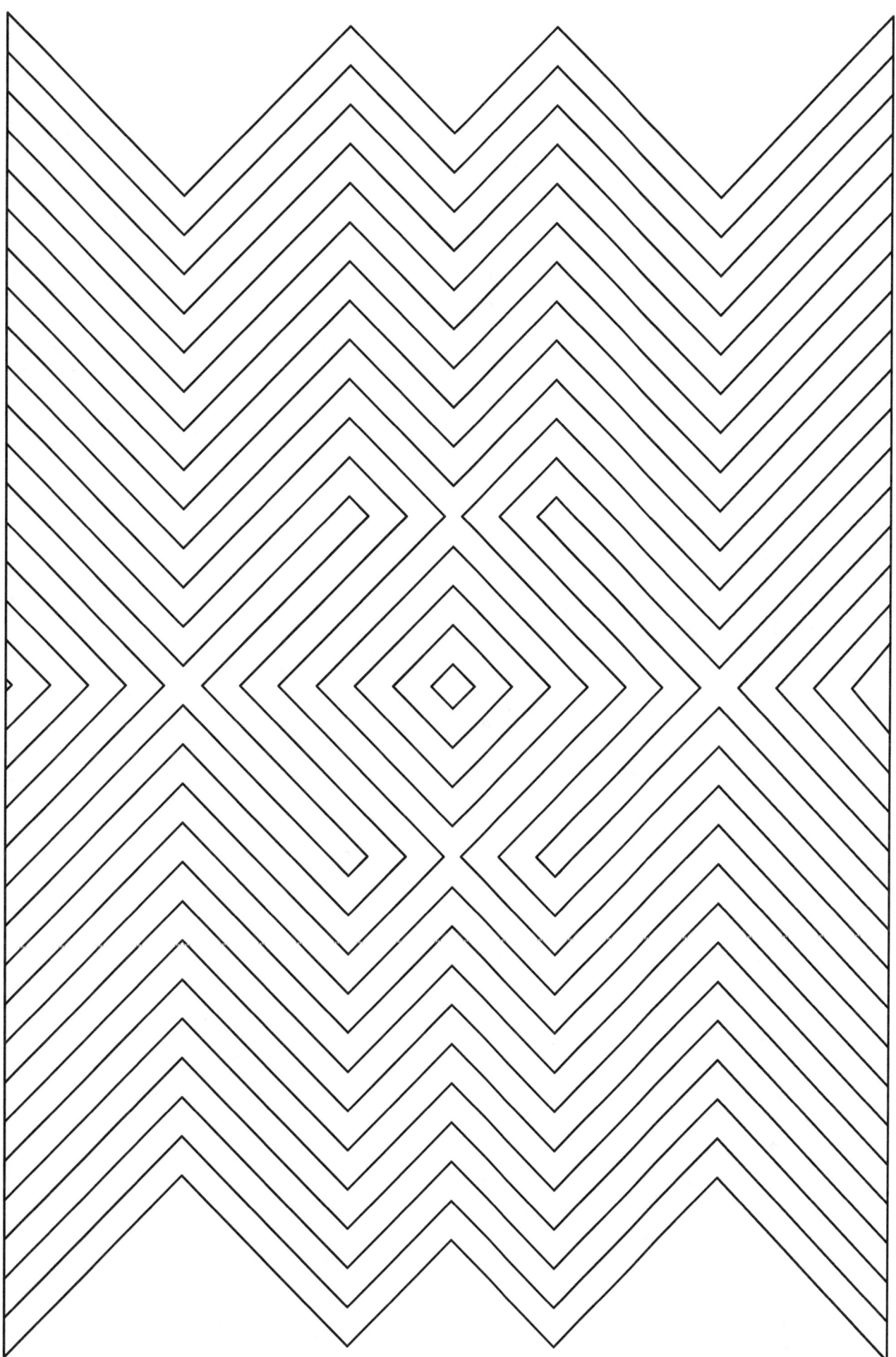

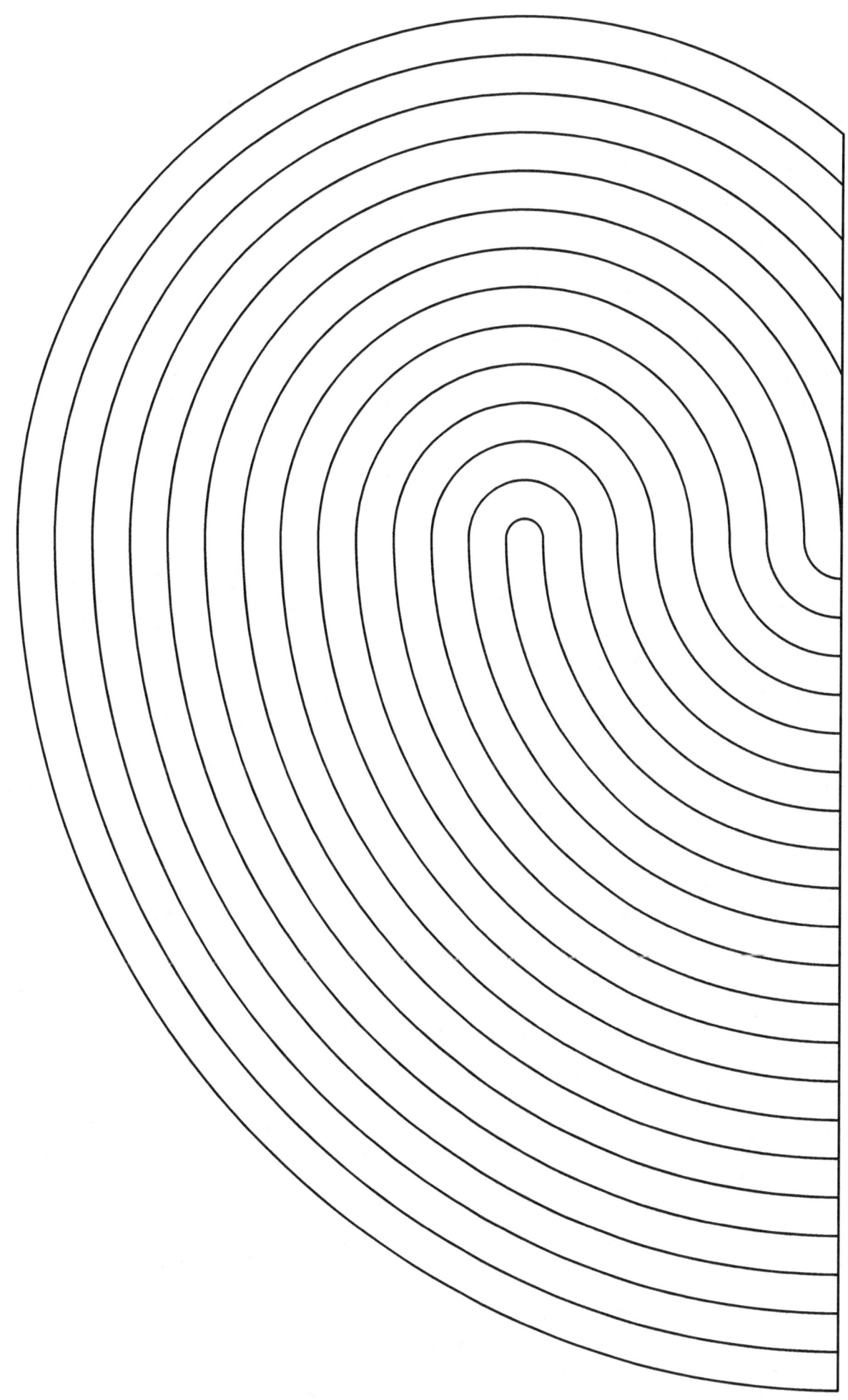

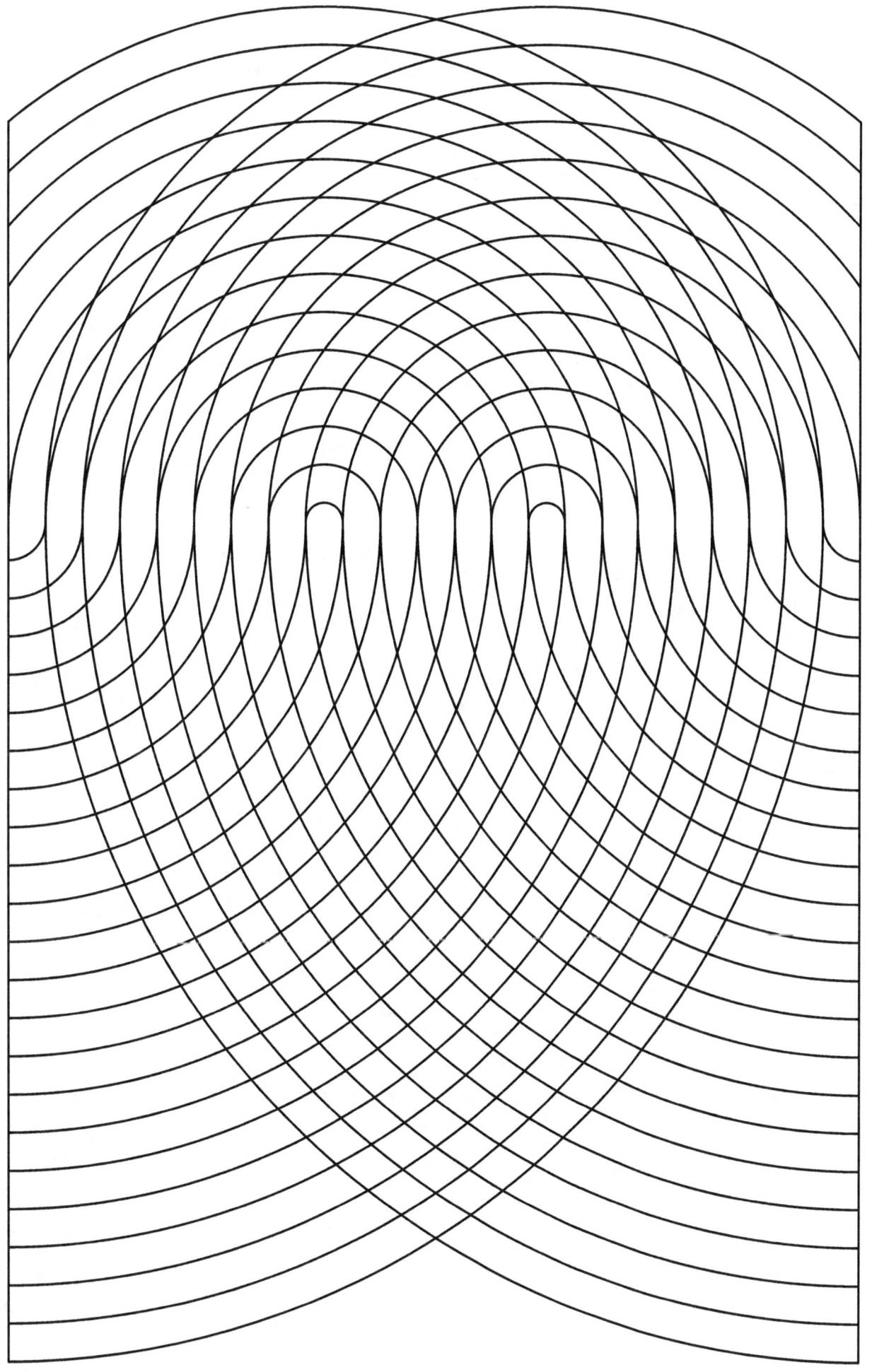

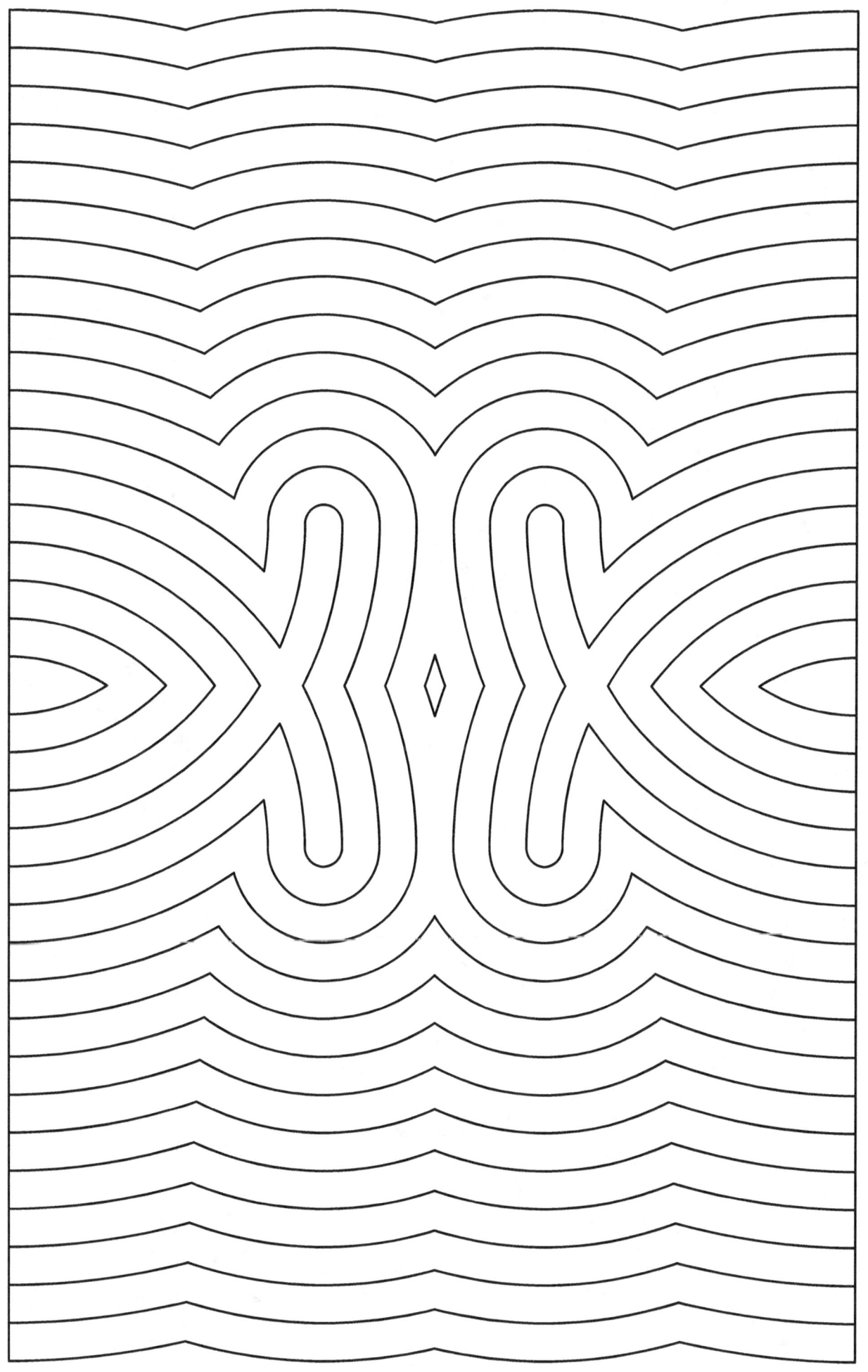

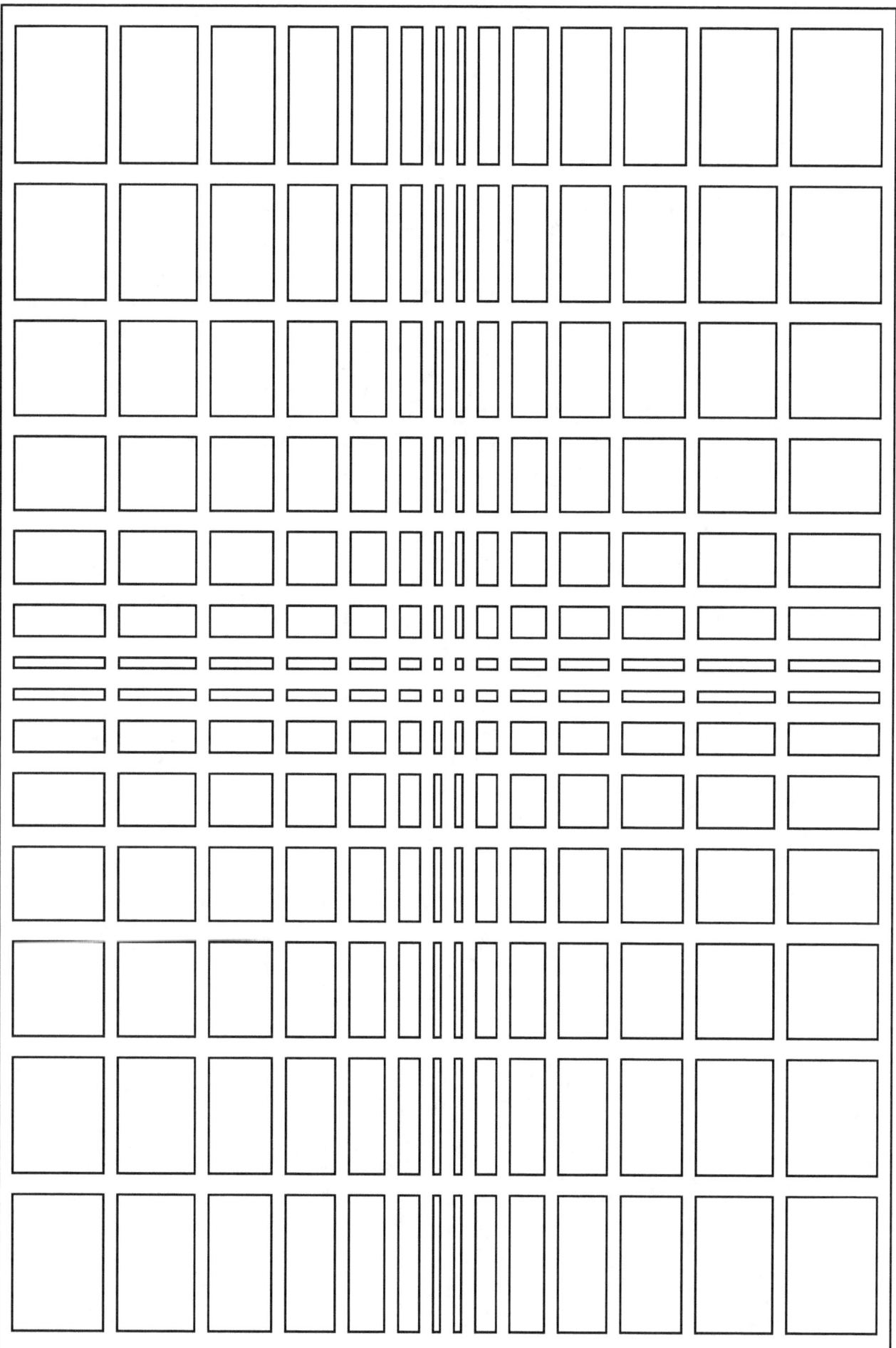

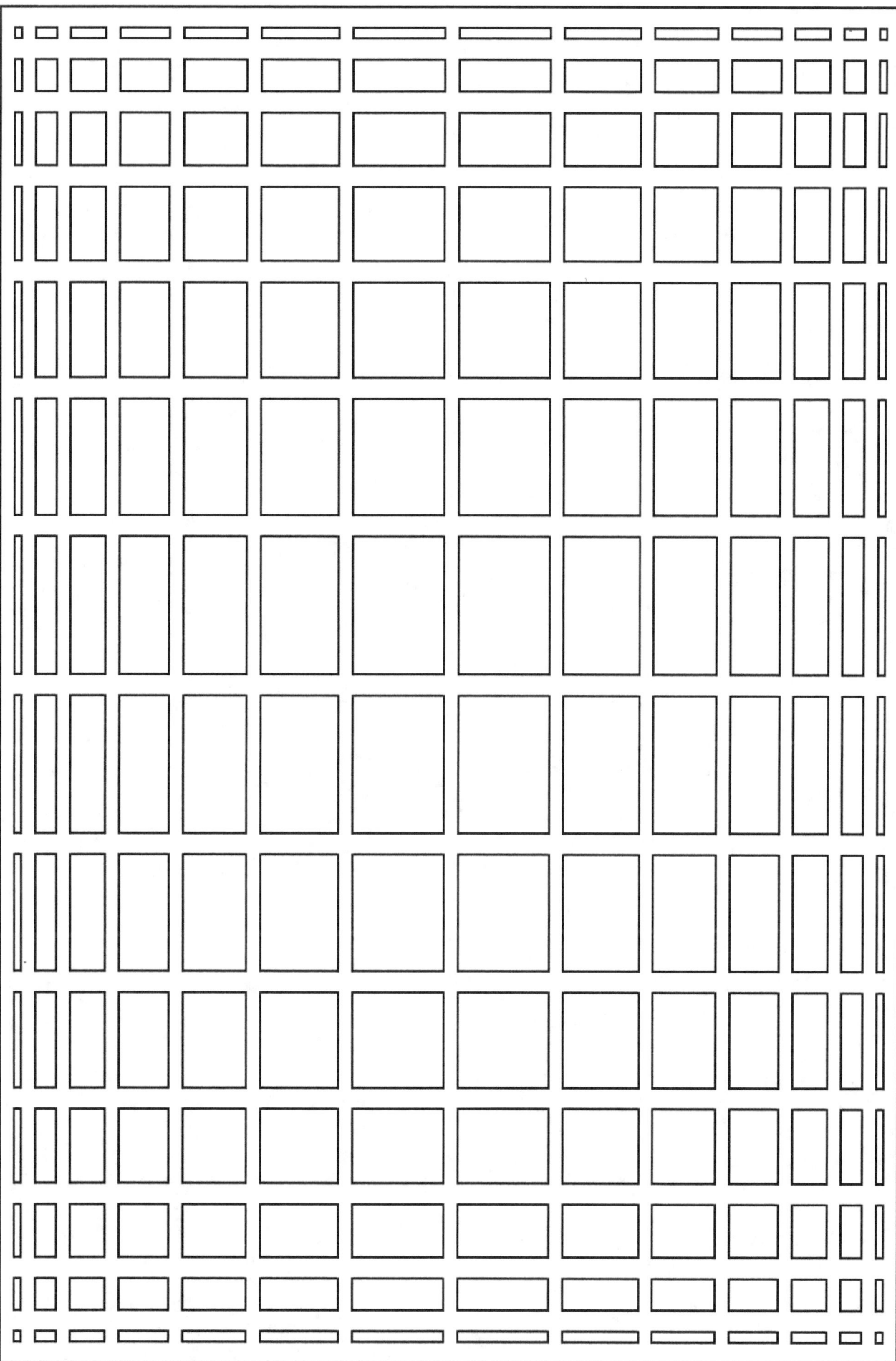

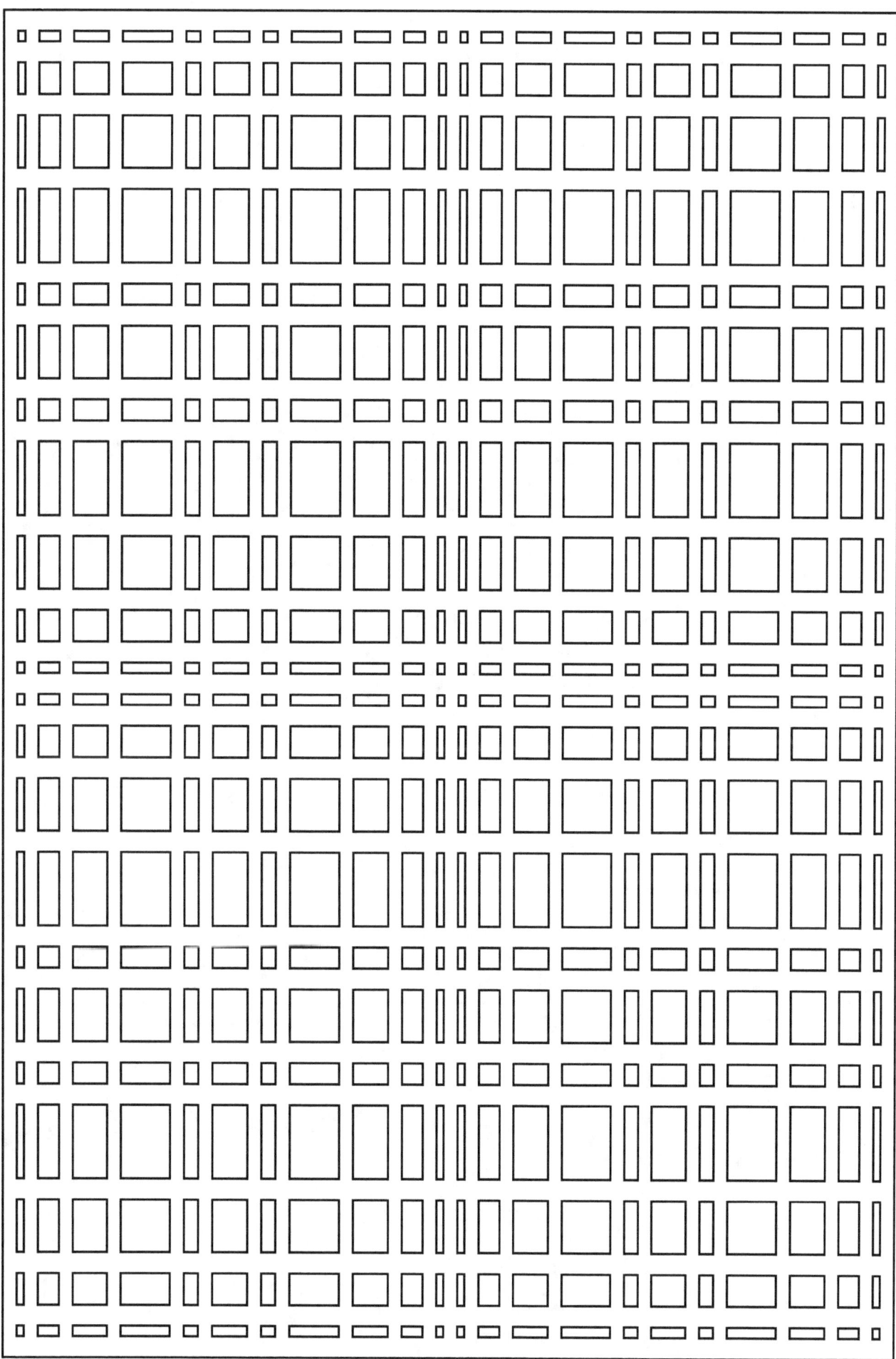

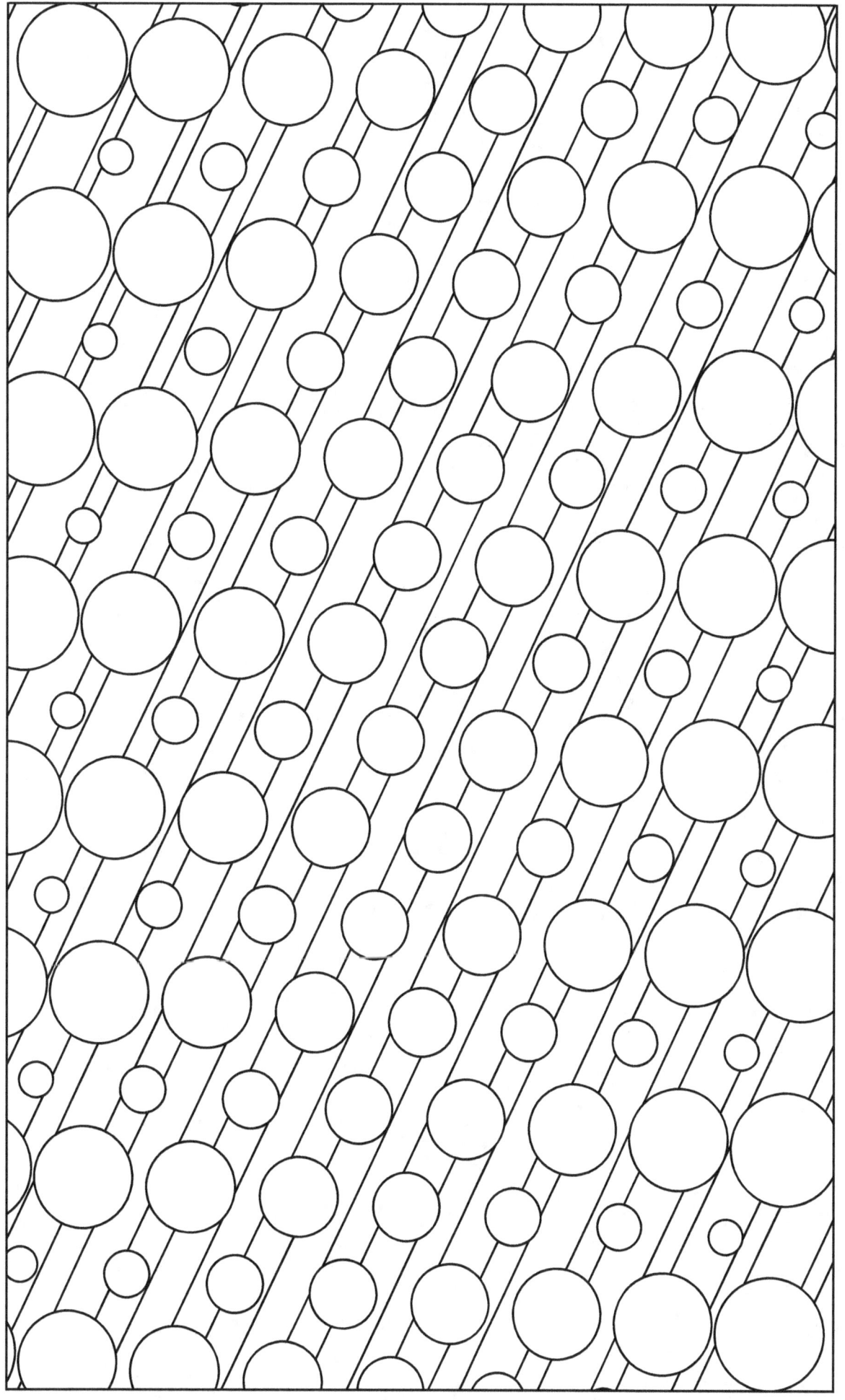

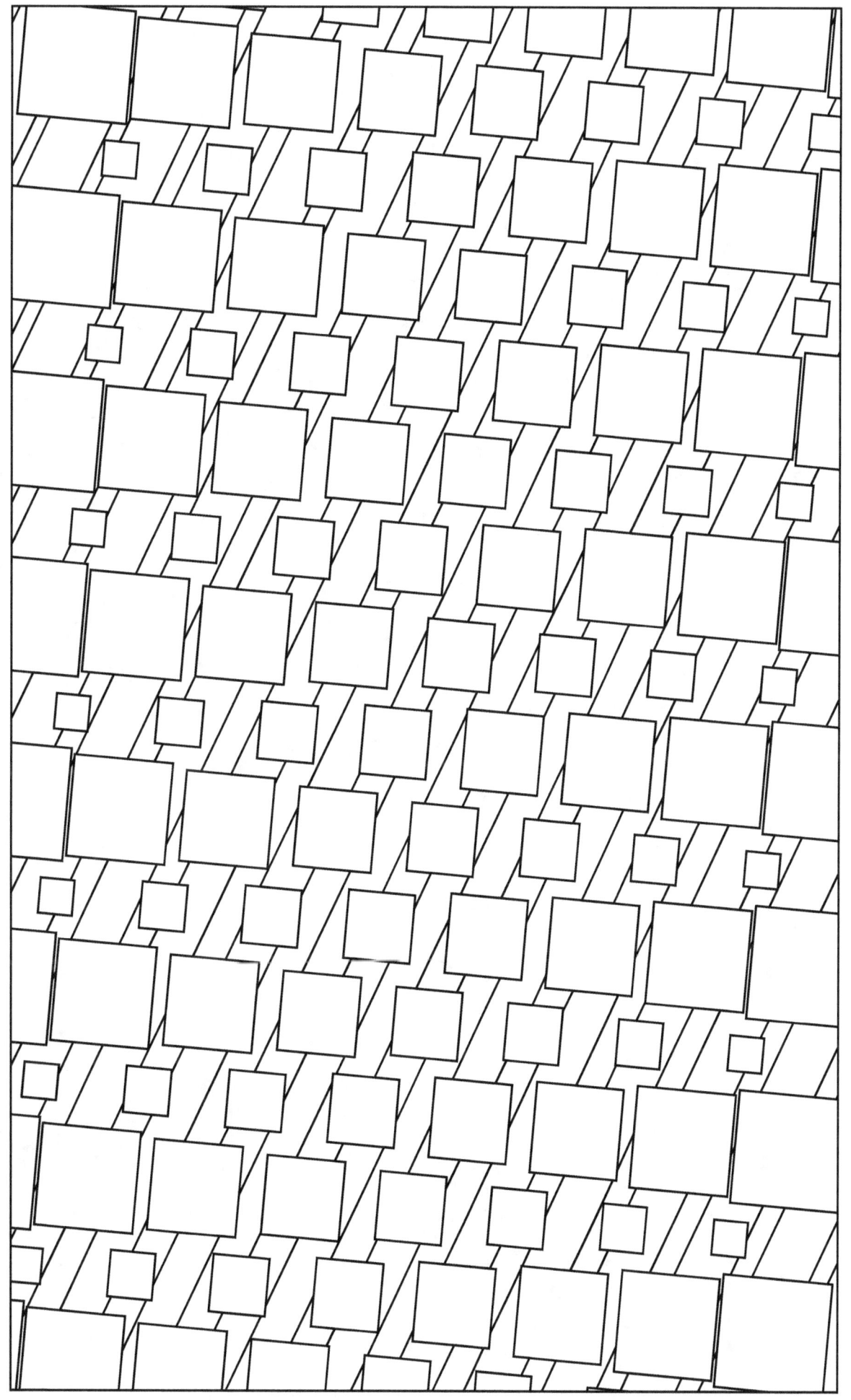

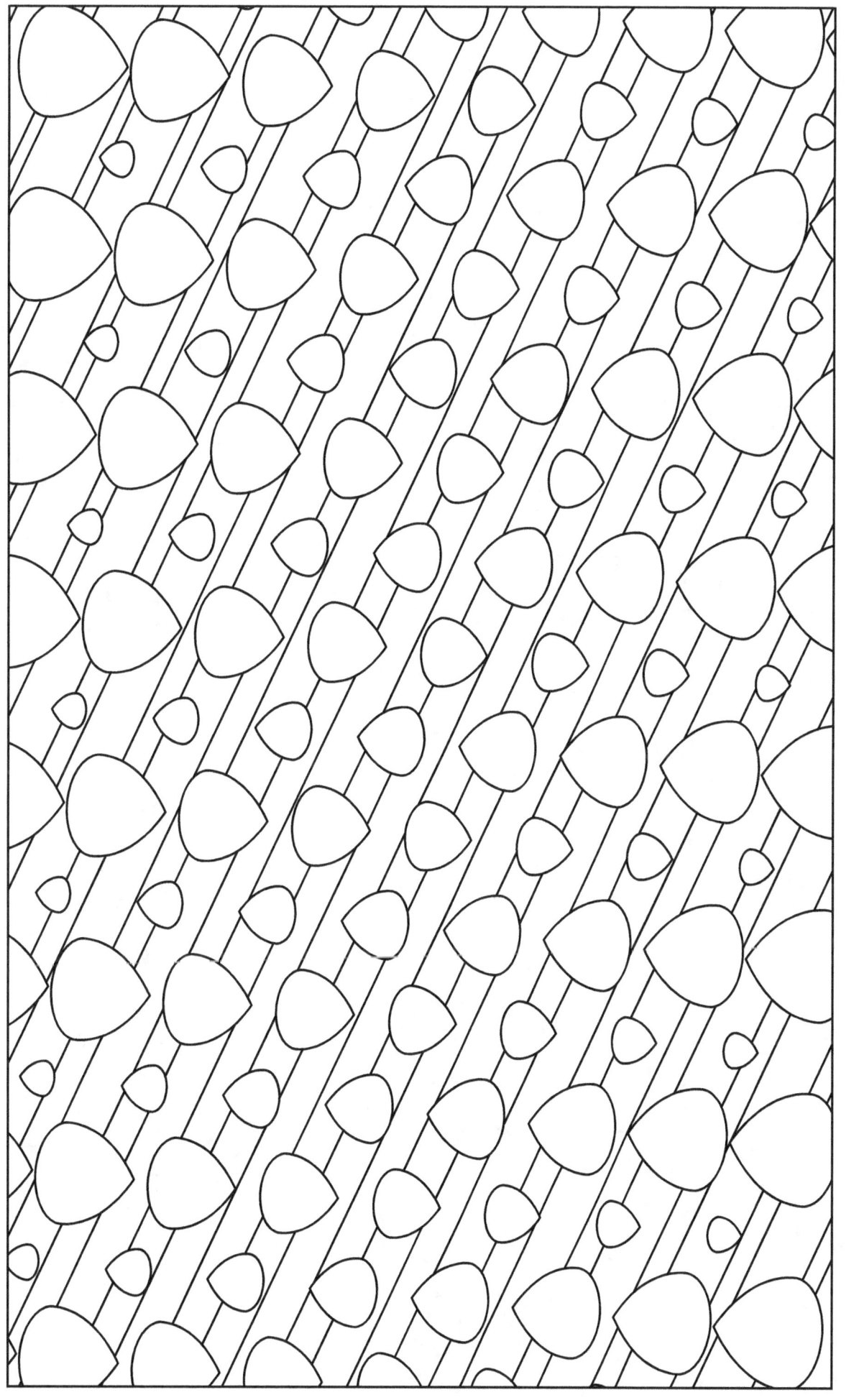

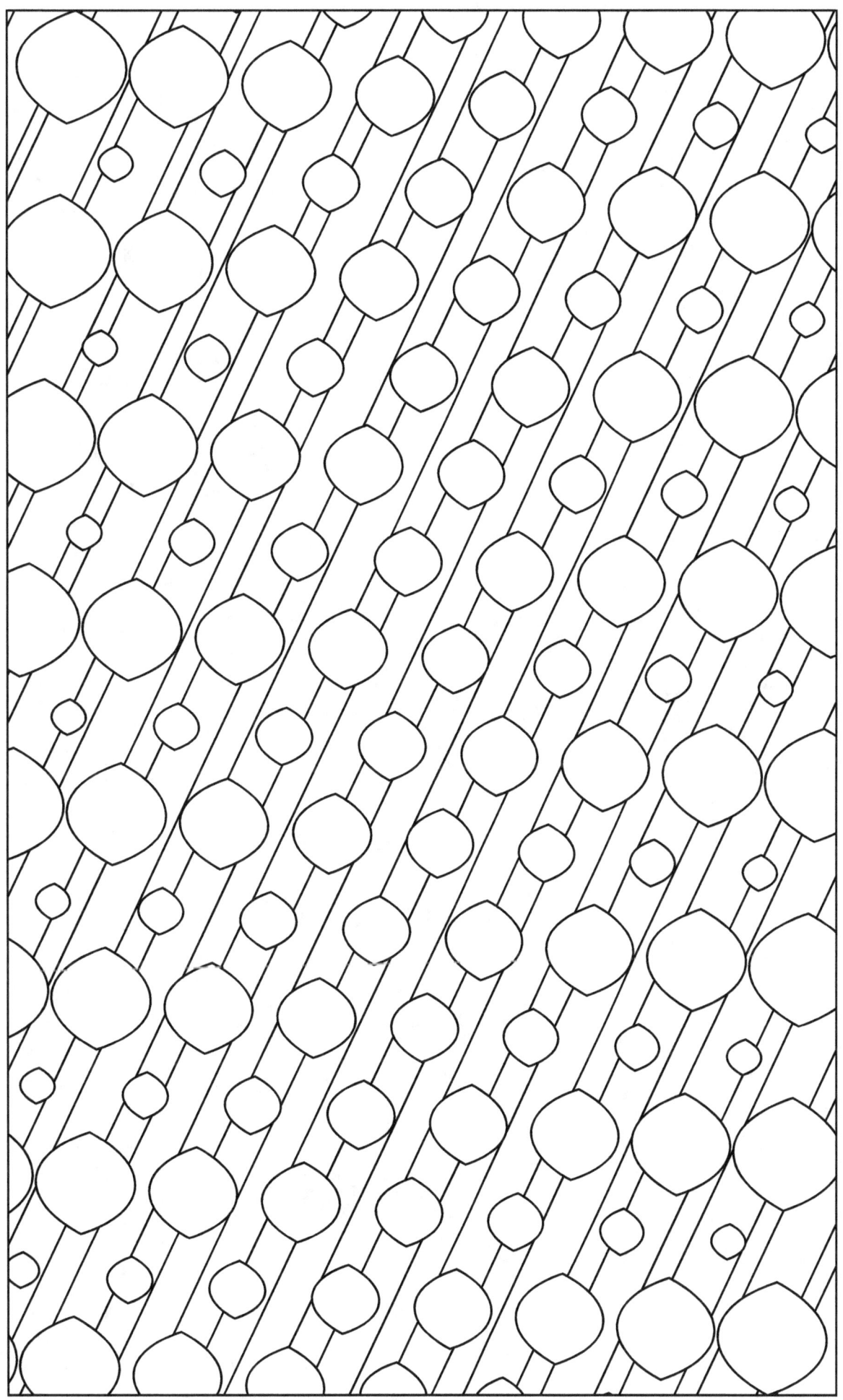

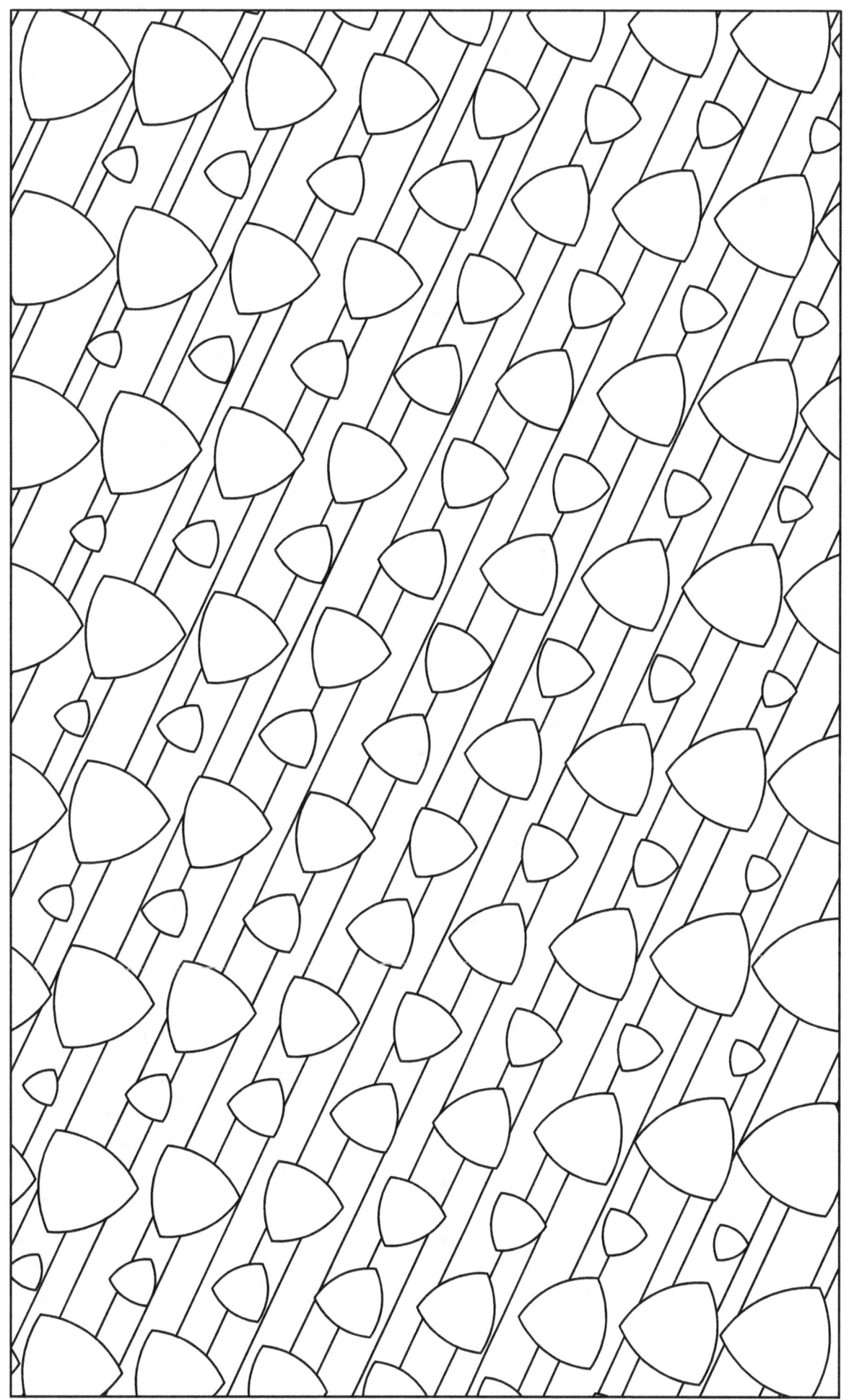

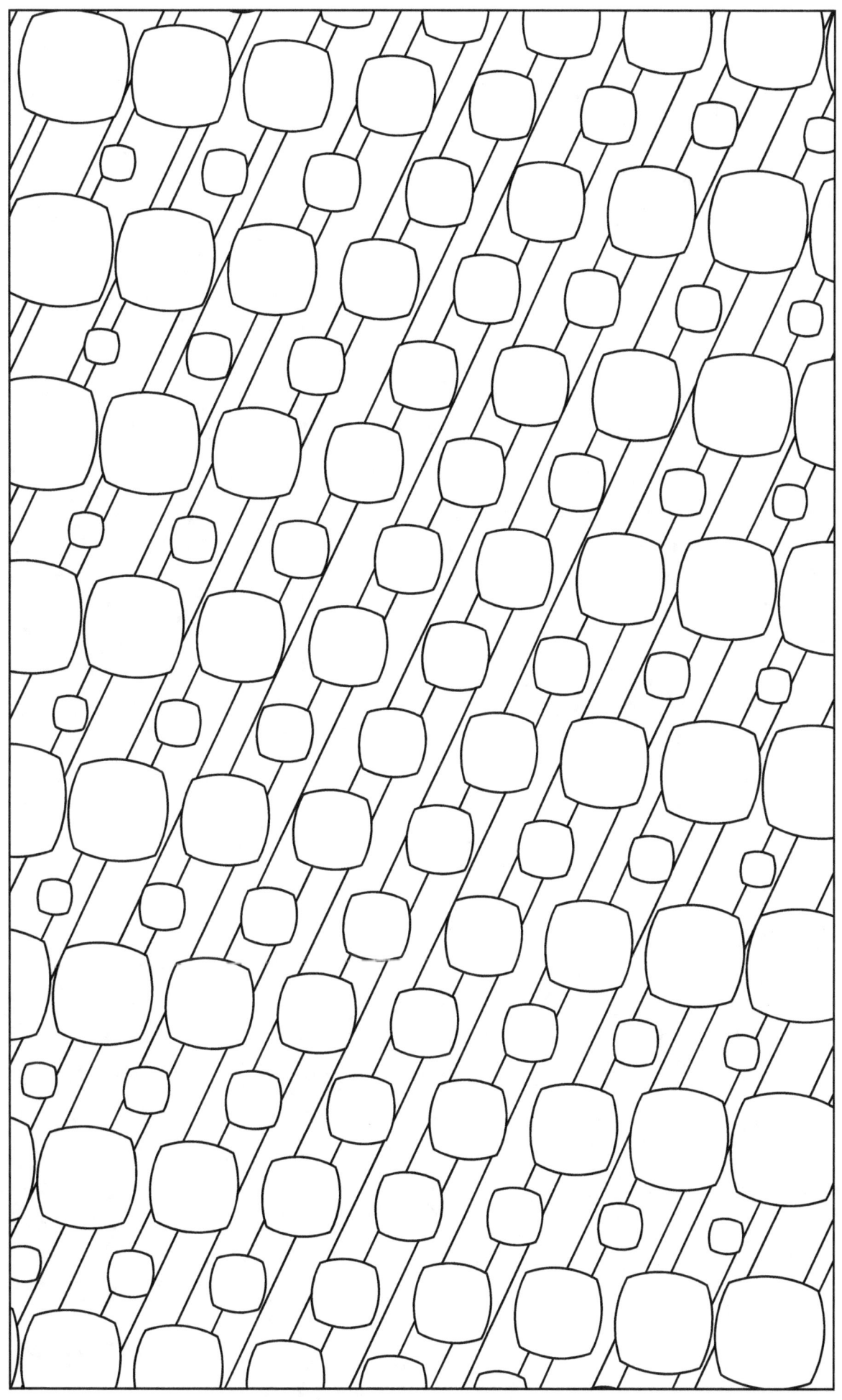

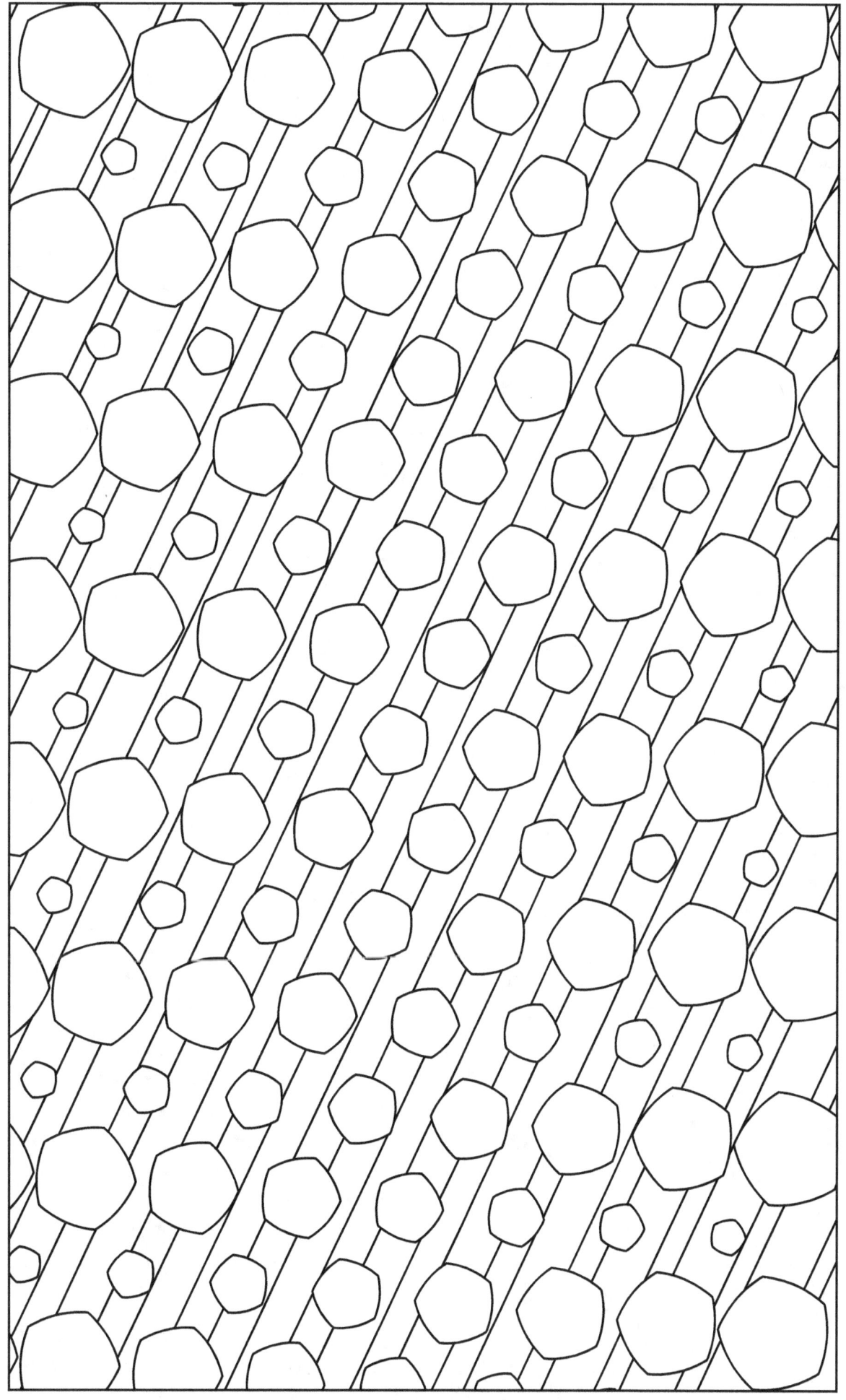

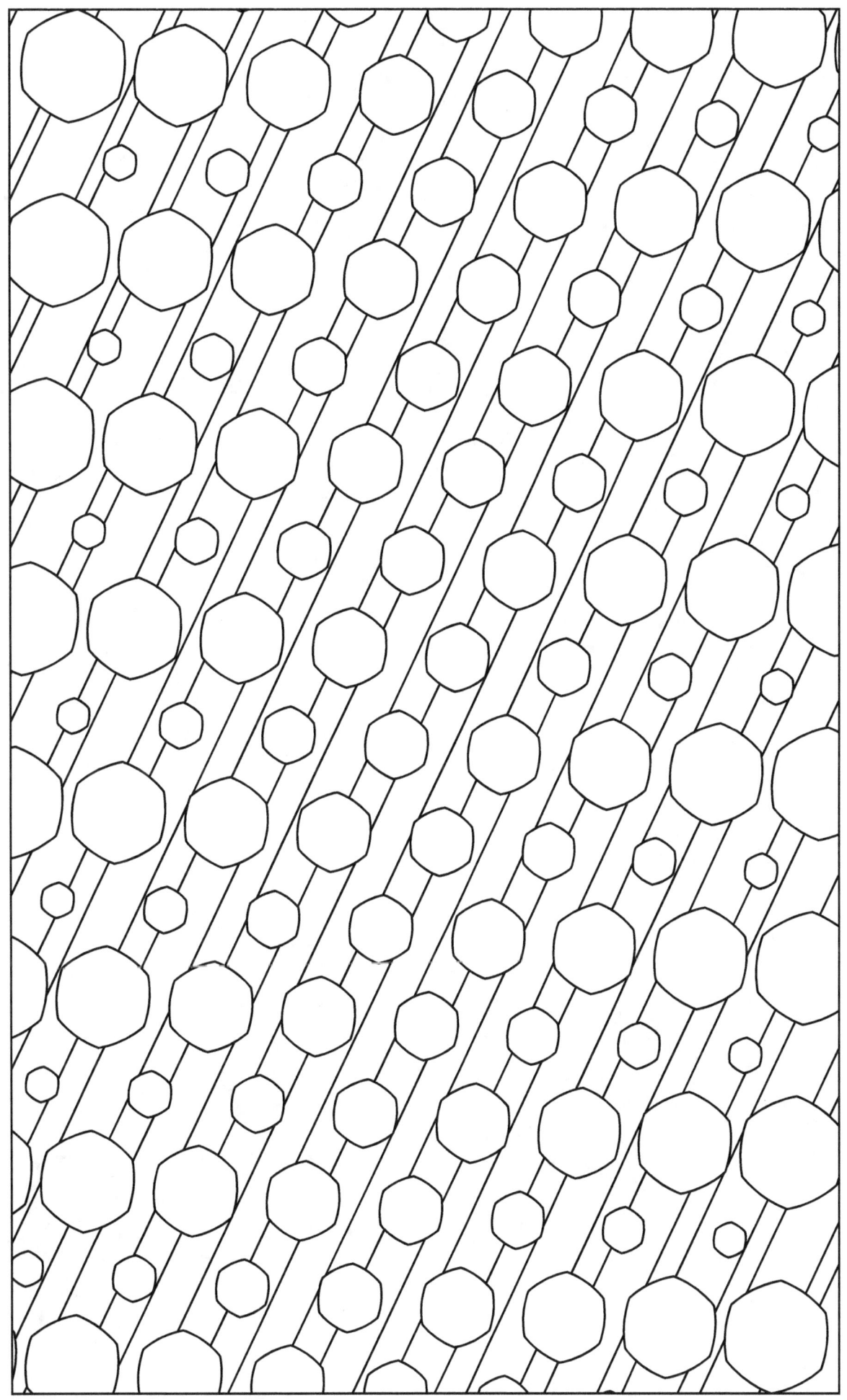

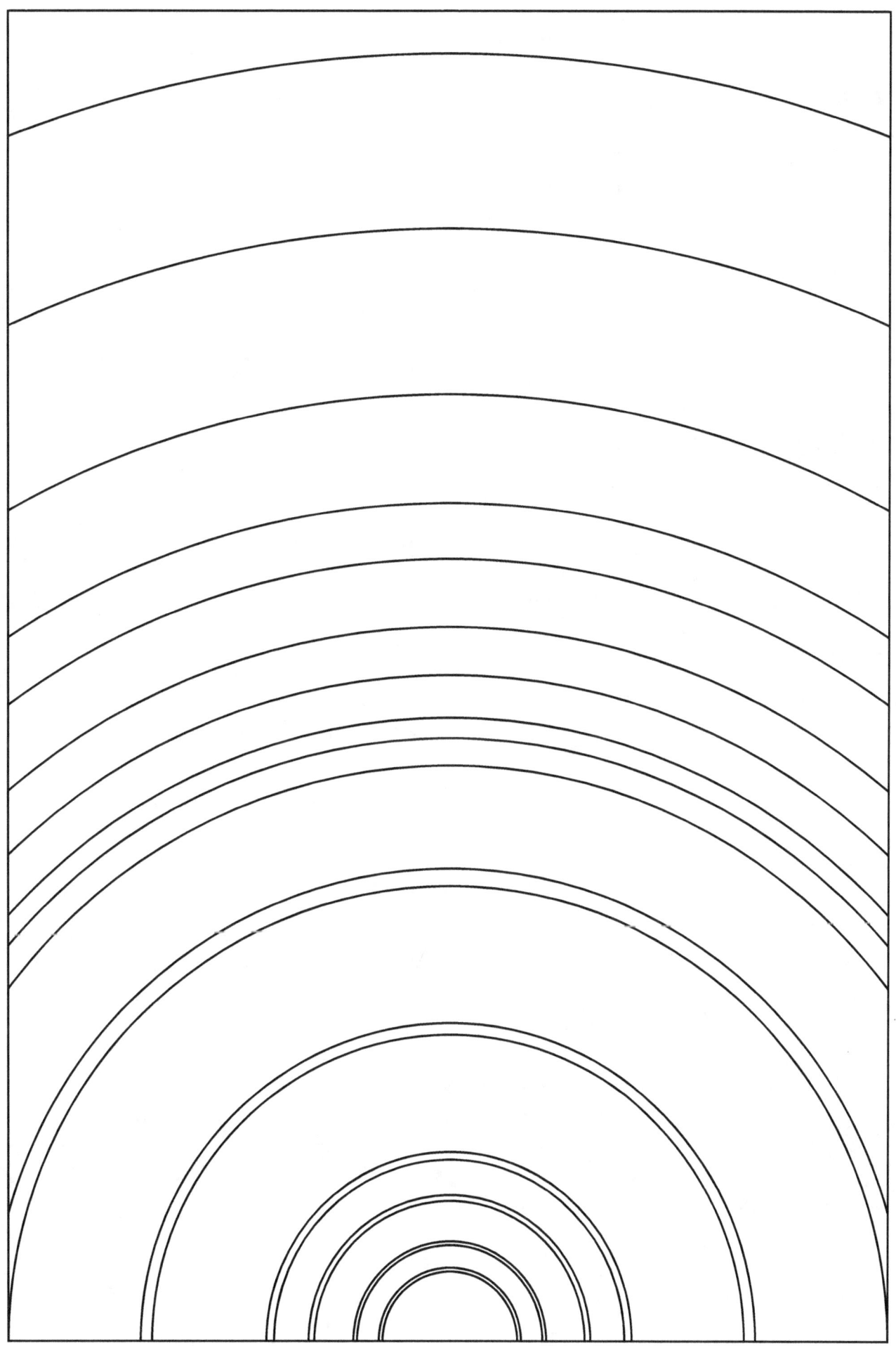

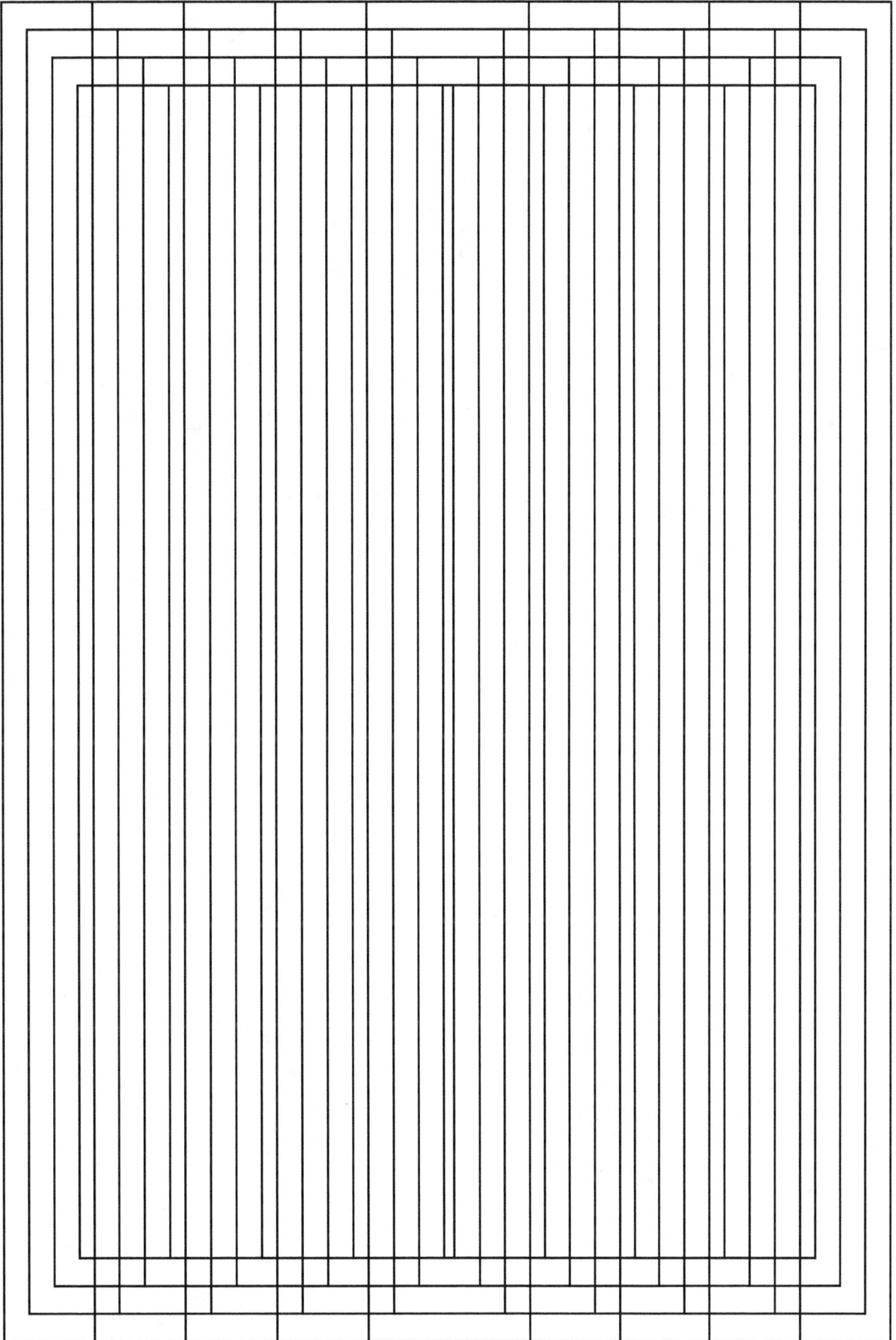

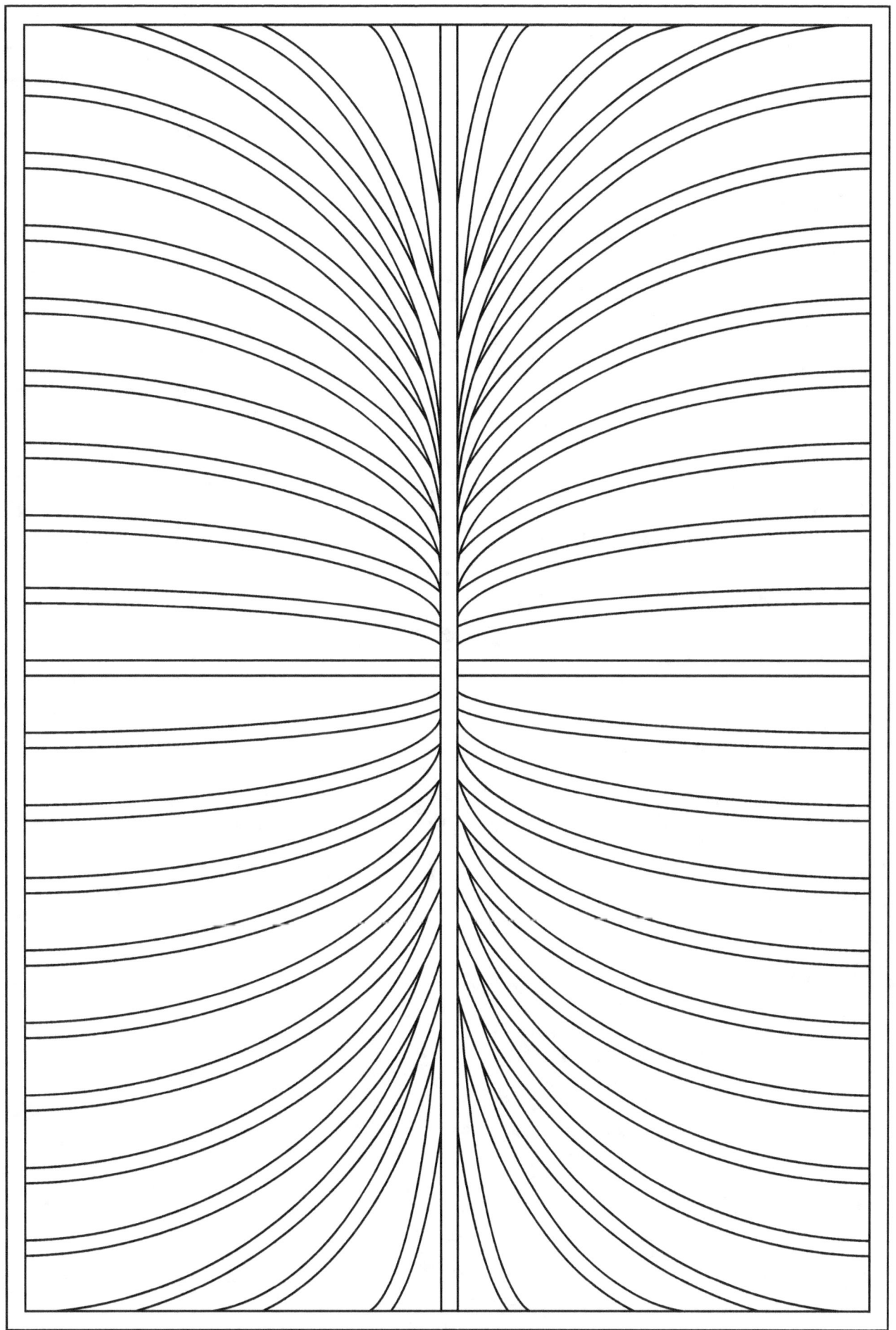

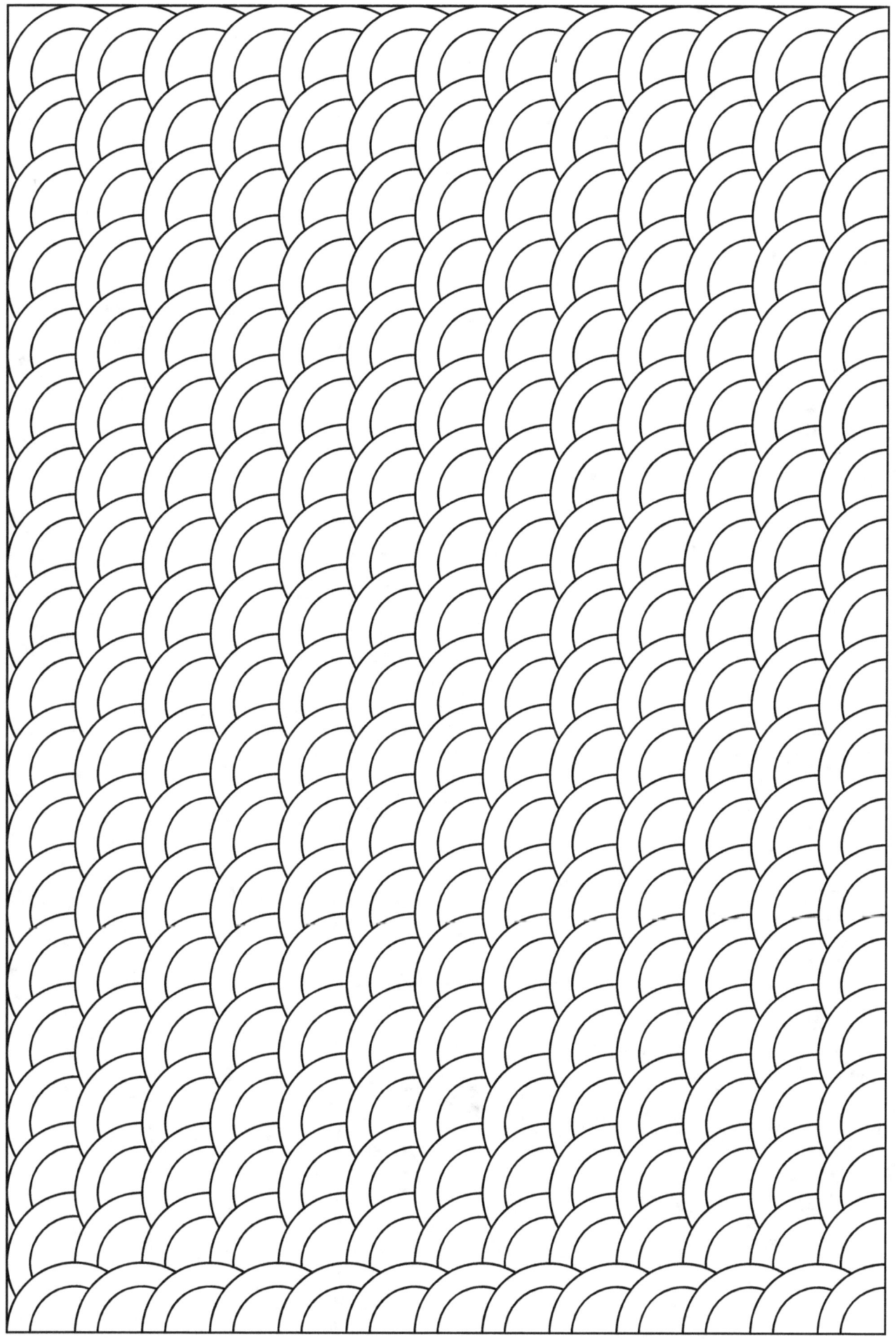

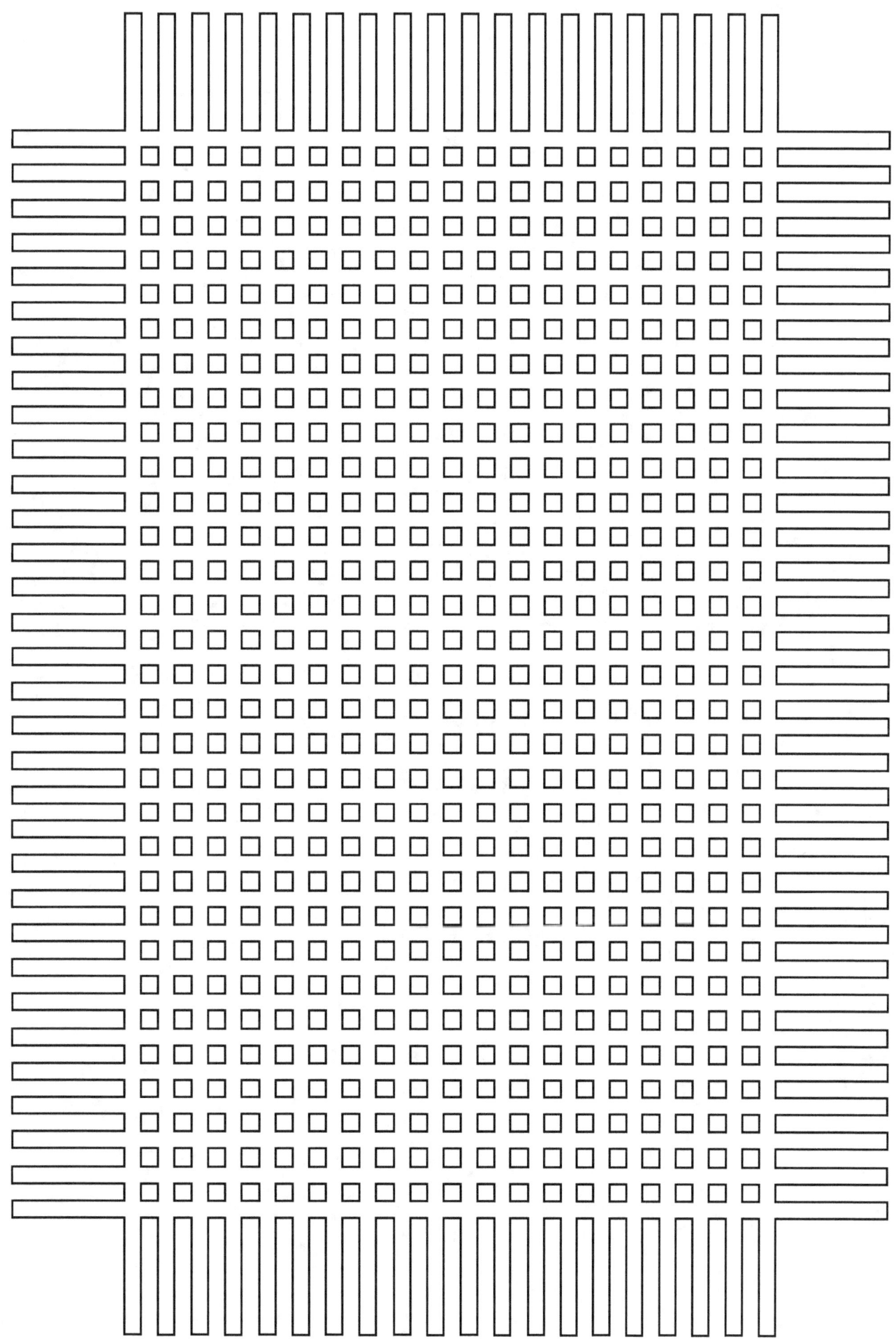

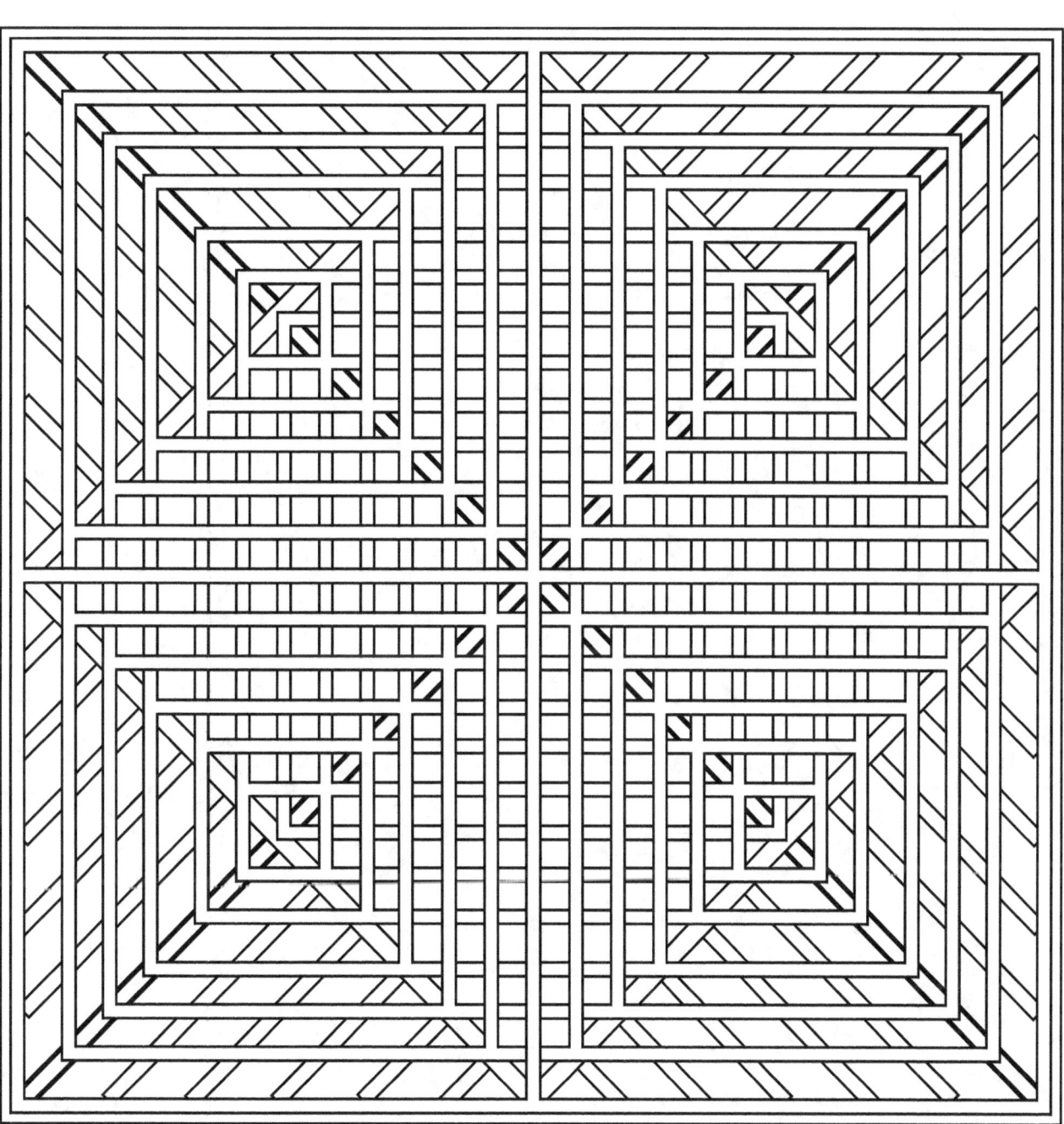

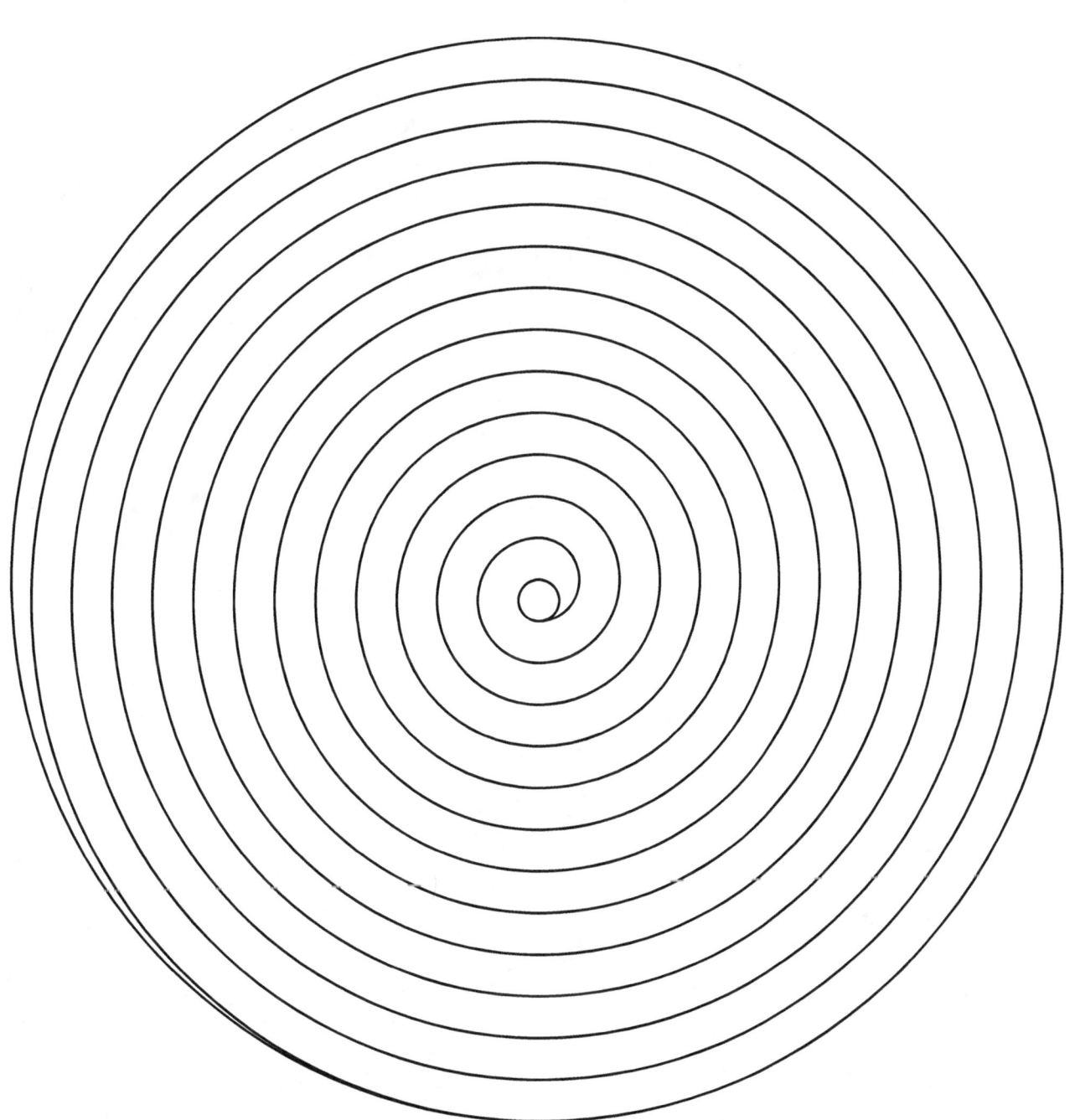

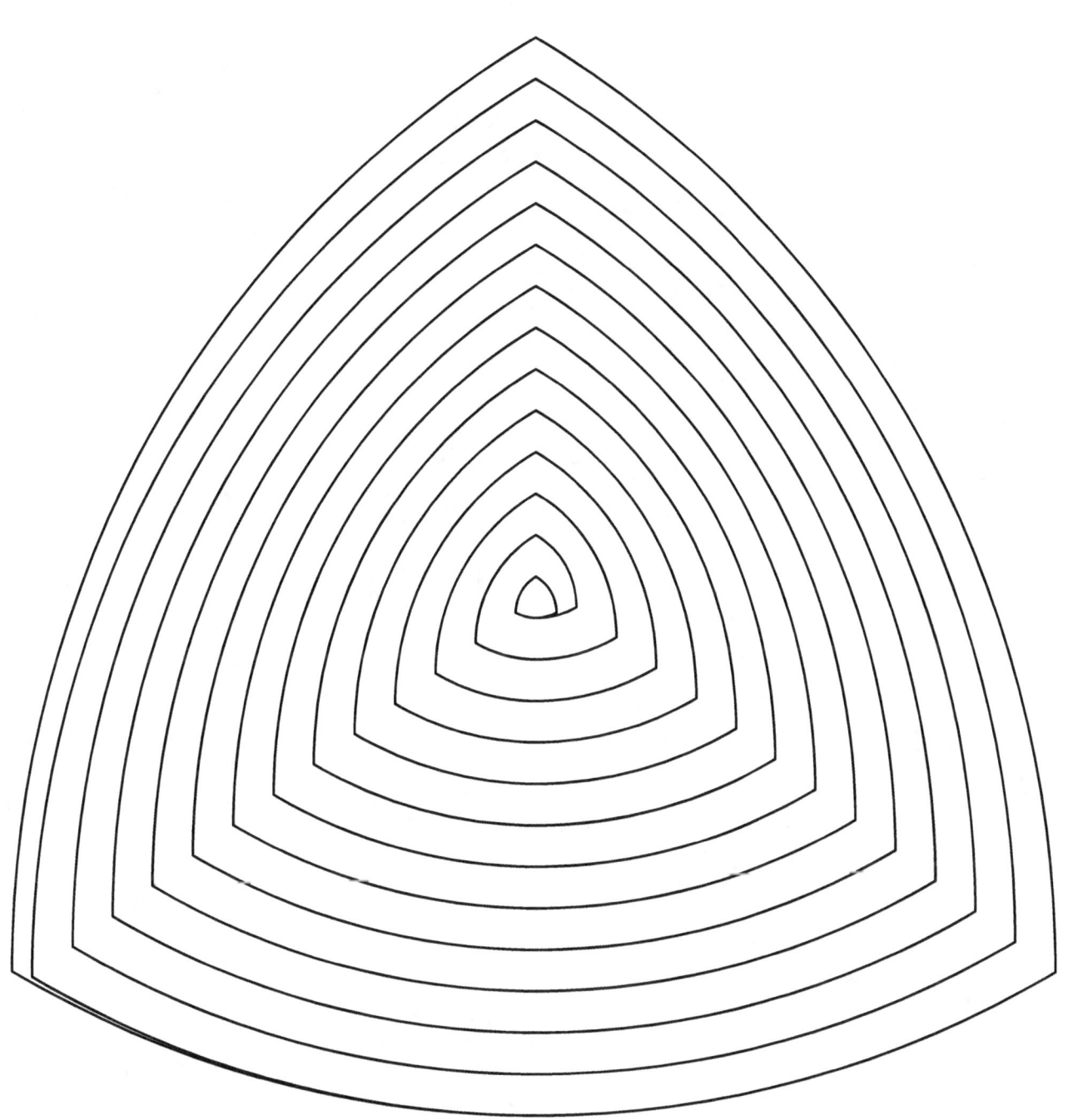

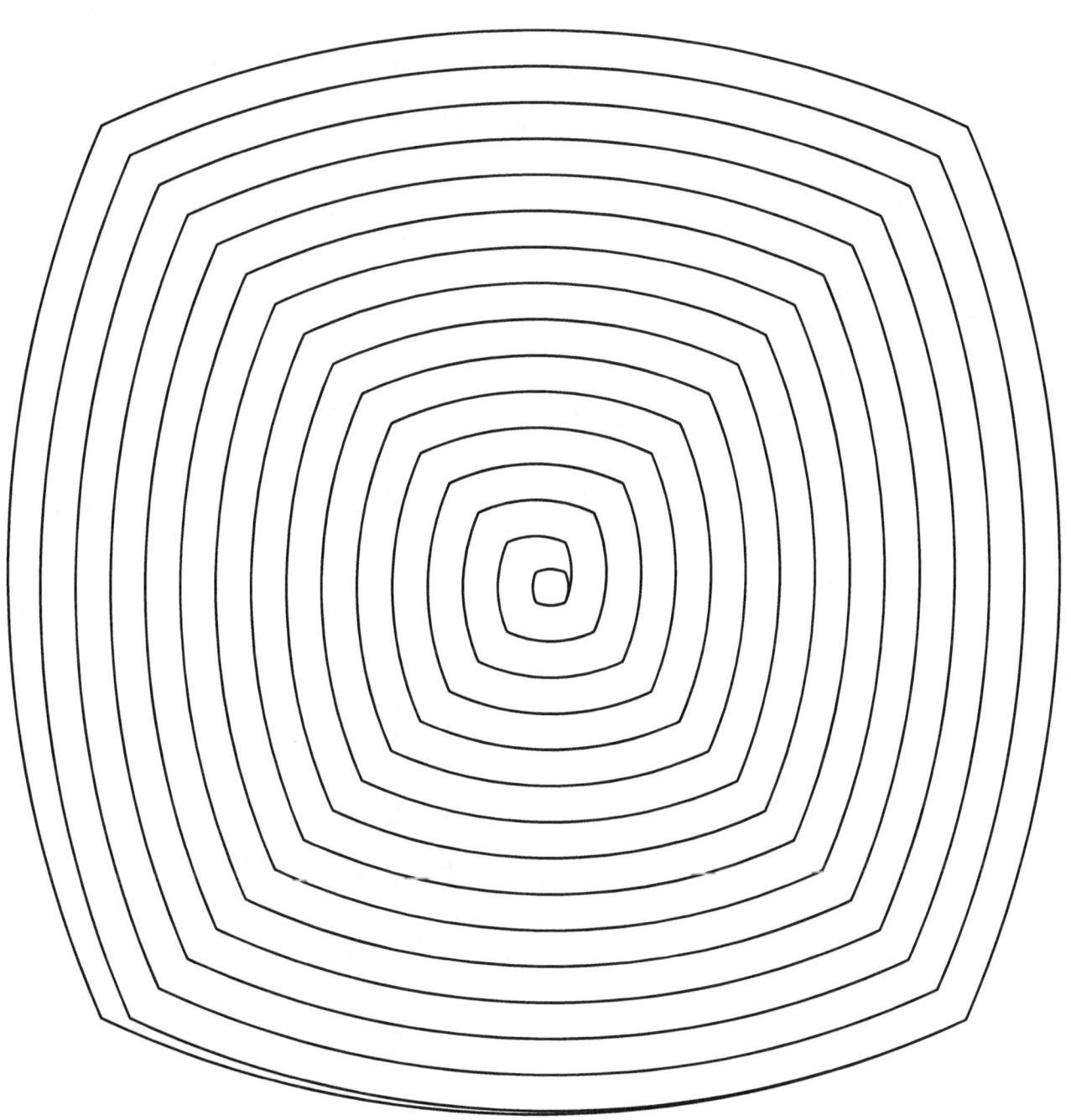

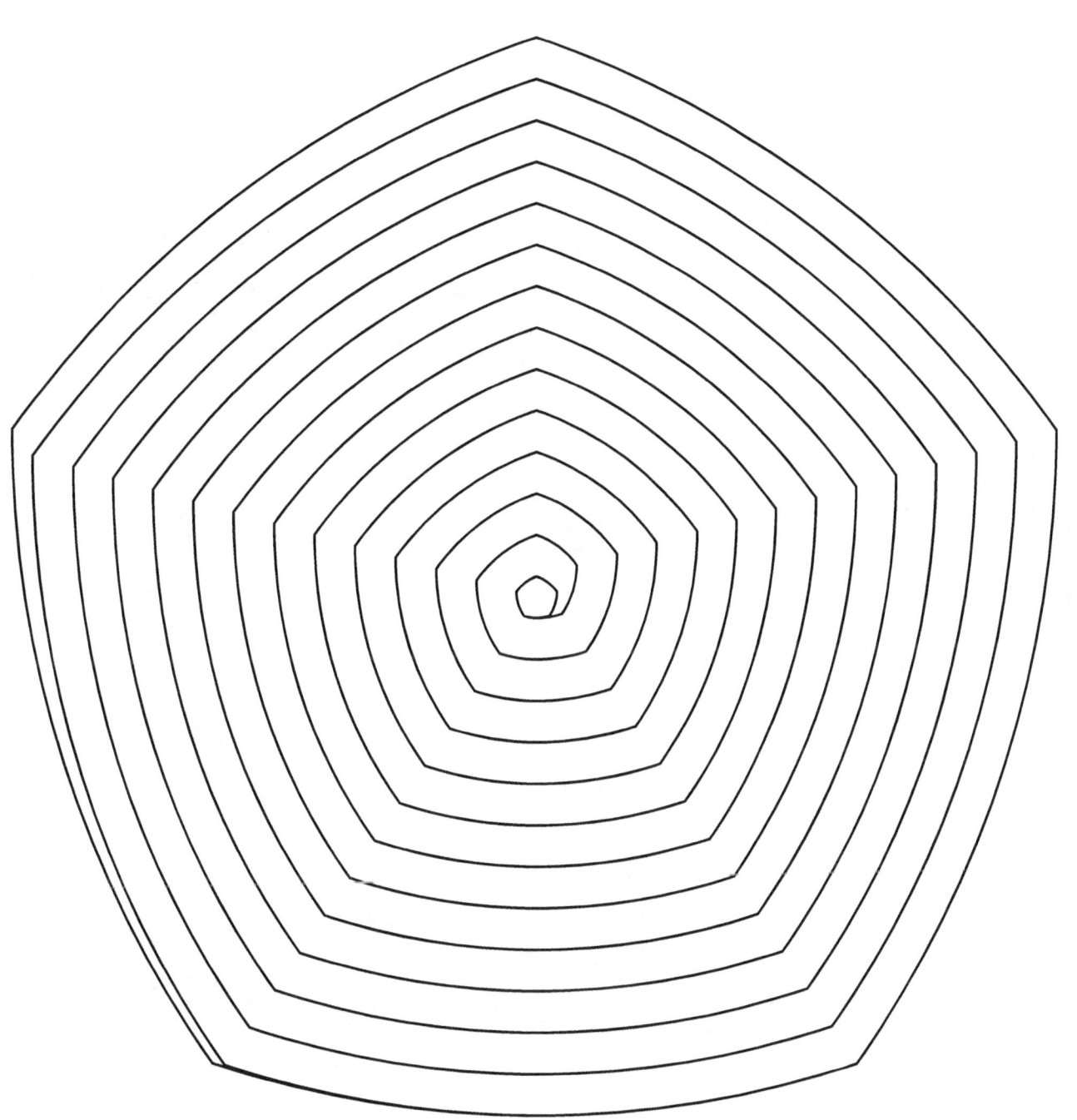

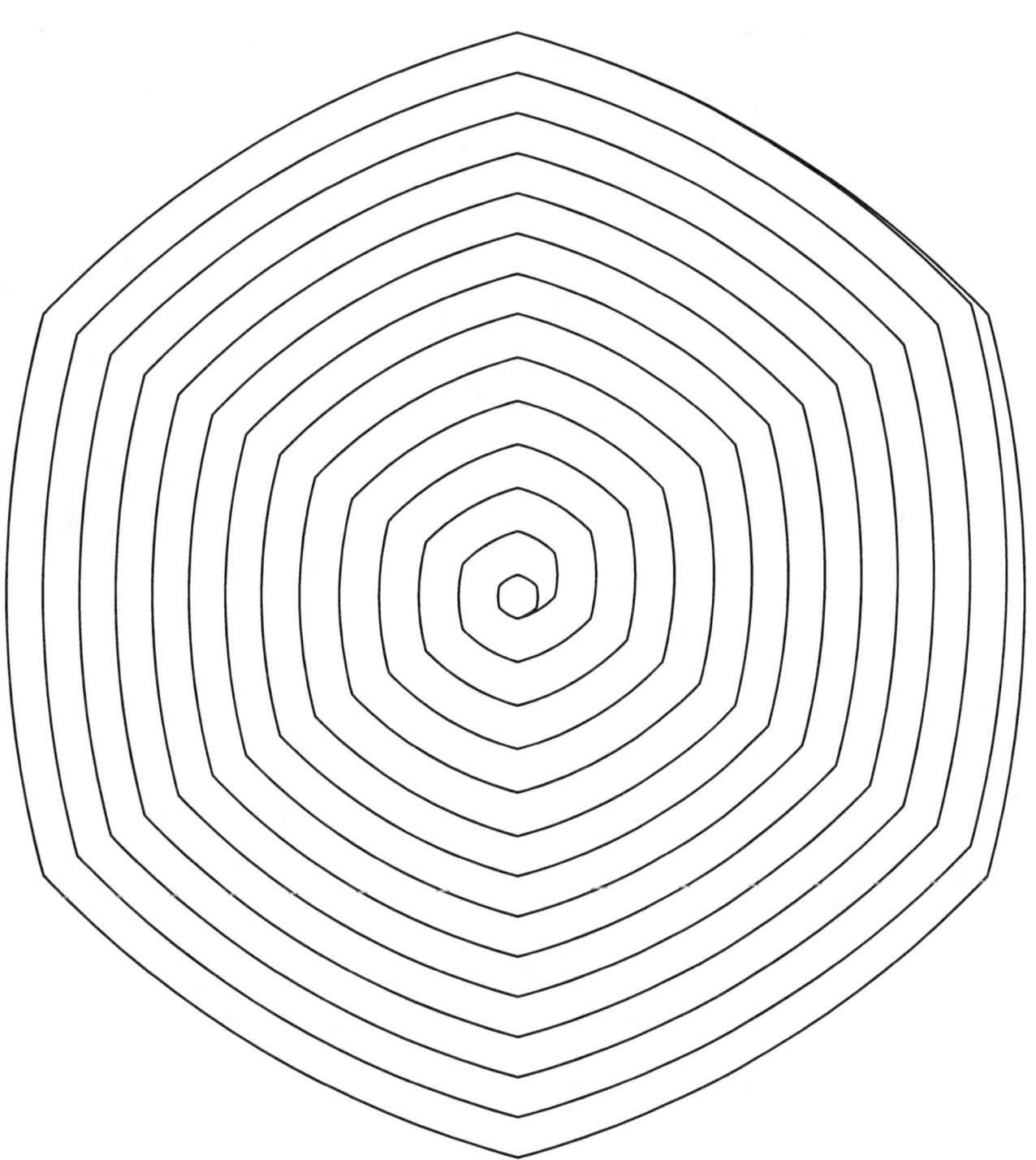

MINIMALIST·DESIGNS·2

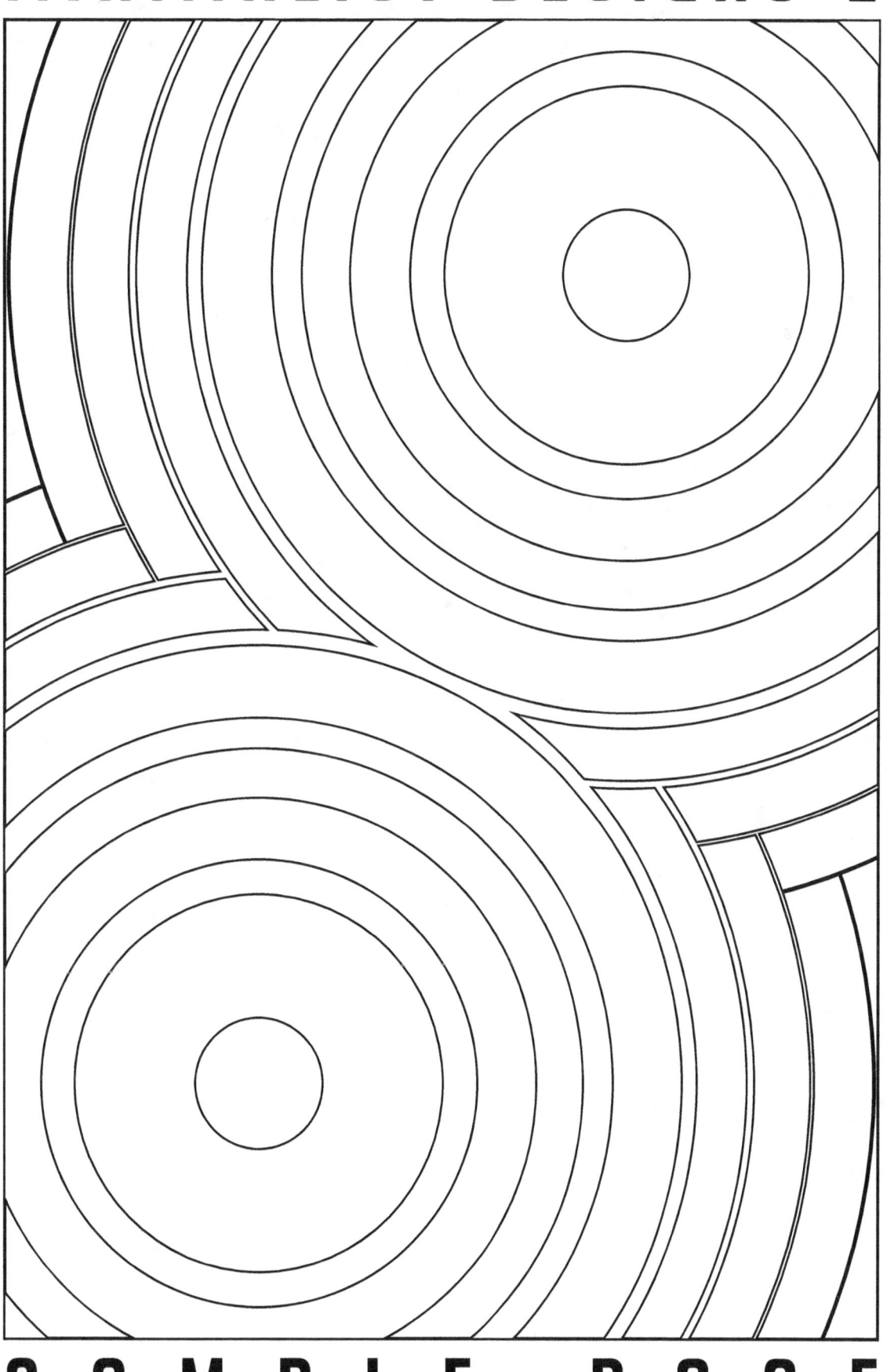

SAMPLE·PAGE

FIBONACCI·DESIGNS·1

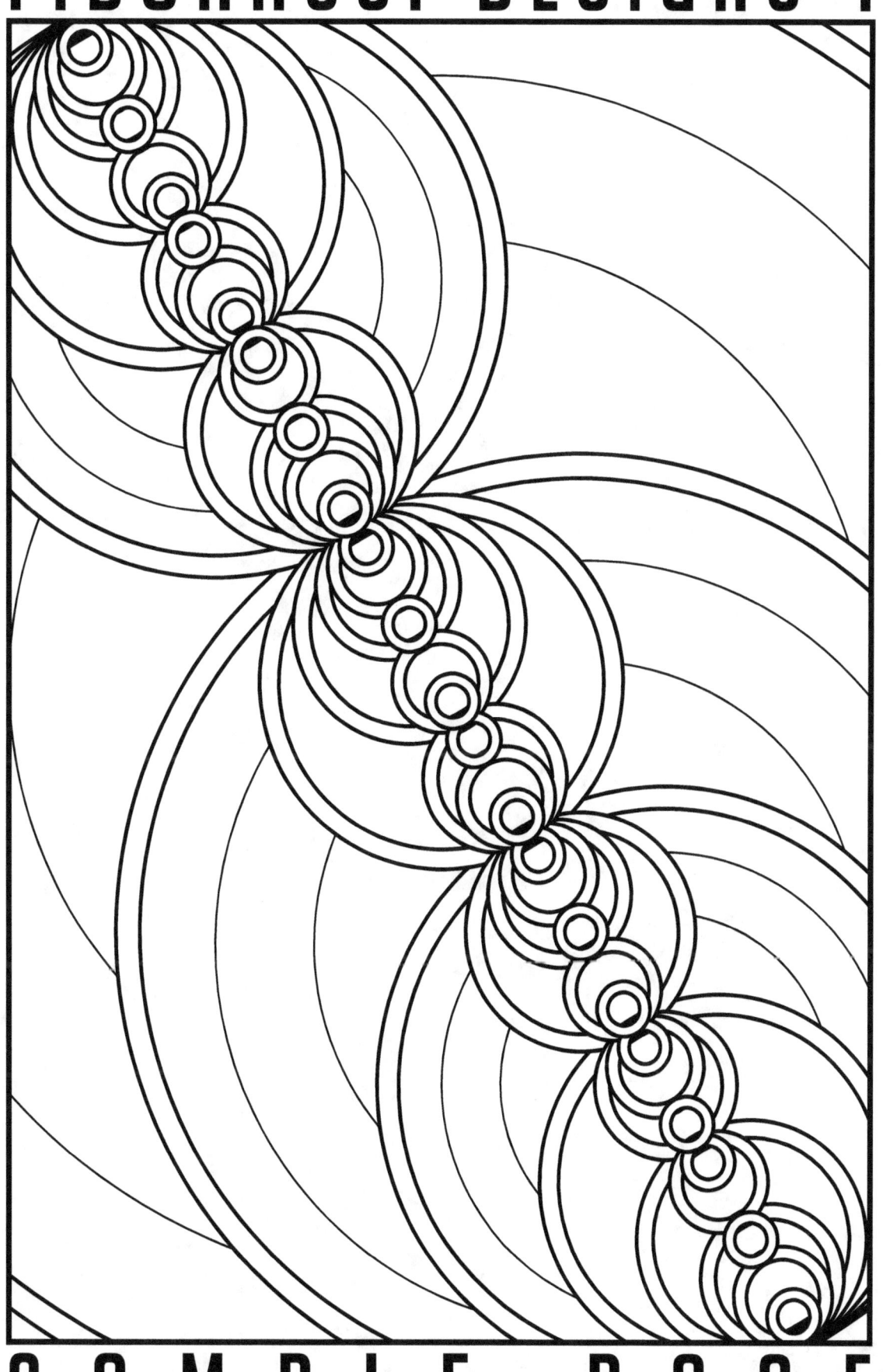

SAMPLE·PAGE

GEOMETRIC·DESIGNS·1

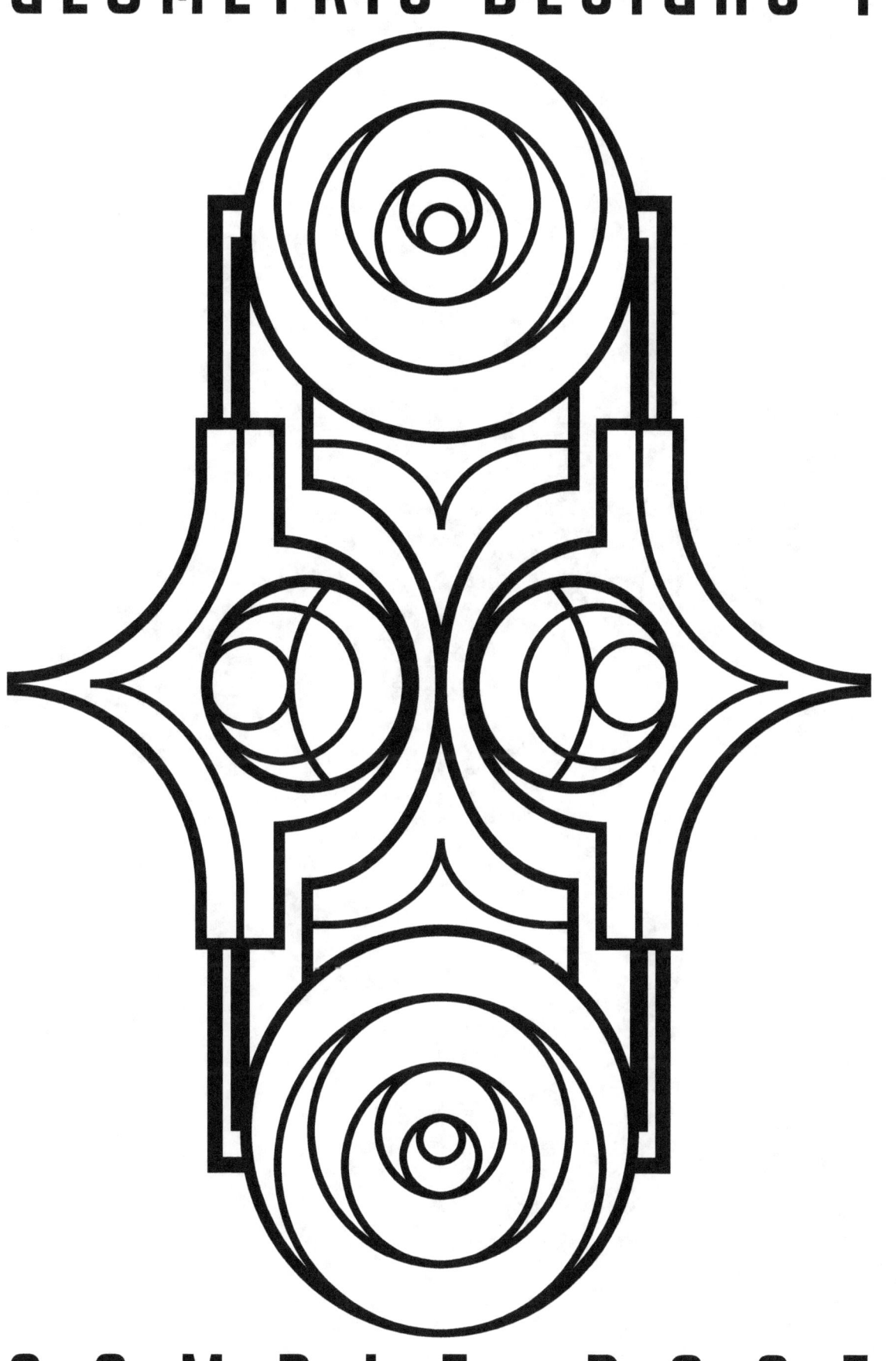

SAMPLE·PAGE

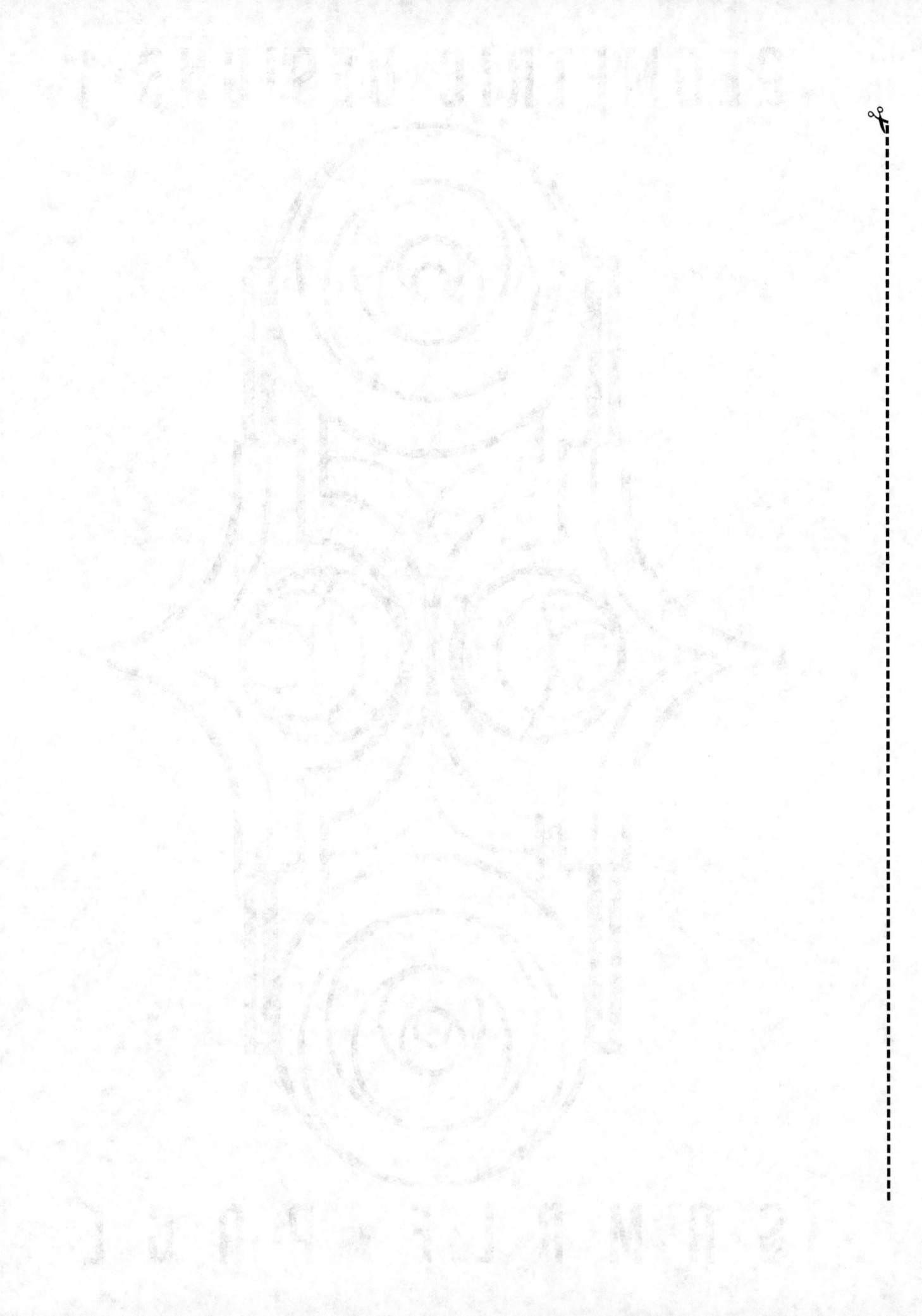

www.ingramcontent.com/pod-product-compliance
Lightning Source LLC
Chambersburg PA
CBHW081527220526
45467CB00010B/3078